SYMPATHY AND ETHICS

Sympathy and Ethics

A STUDY OF THE RELATIONSHIP
BETWEEN SYMPATHY AND MORALITY
WITH SPECIAL REFERENCE TO
HUME'S *TREATISE*

PHILIP MERCER

OXFORD
AT THE CLARENDON PRESS
1972

Oxford University Press, Ely House, London W. 1

GLASGOW   NEW YORK   TORONTO   MELBOURNE   WELLINGTON
CAPE TOWN   IBADAN   NAIROBI   DAR ES SALAAM   LUSAKA   ADDIS ABABA
DELHI   BOMBAY   CALCUTTA   MADRAS   KARACHI   LAHORE   DACCA
KUALA LUMPUR   SINGAPORE   HONG KONG   TOKYO

PRINTED IN GREAT BRITAIN
AT THE UNIVERSITY PRESS, OXFORD
BY VIVIAN RIDLER
PRINTER TO THE UNIVERSITY

PREFACE

My ideas on sympathy have been stimulated by many writers from David Hume onwards—their names are mentioned in the text and I am deeply in their debt. In addition, I particularly wish to express my gratitude to my friend and teacher, Dr. D. O. Thomas of Aberystwyth, for all the discussions we have had together and for the advice and help he has given me. I should also like to thank Professor R. I. Aaron for his encouragement while this book was in preparation. Dr. Páll S. Árdal of Edinburgh very kindly read the entire typescript and I am greatly indebted to him for his numerous valuable suggestions and corrections.

Blackheath, London   P. C. M.

January 1971

CONTENTS

CONTENTS

ABBREVIATIONS

'E.I.S.'   H. B. Acton, 'The Ethical Importance of Sympathy',
            Philosophy (1955).
F.T.E.T.   C. D. Broad, *Five Types of Ethical Theory*, Routledge &
            Kegan Paul, London 1930.
G.M.M.   Immanuel Kant, *Groundwork of the Metaphysics of Morals*,
            in *The Moral Law*, translated by H. J. Paton, Hutchinson,
            London 1956.
N.S.   Max Scheler, *The Nature of Sympathy*, translated by P. L.
            Heath, Routledge & Kegan Paul, London 1954.
P.V.H.T.   Páll S. Árdal, *Passion and Value in Hume's Treatise*, Uni-
            versity Press, Edinburgh 1966.
R.C.H.T.   Rachael M. Kydd, *Reason and Conduct in Hume's Treatise*
            Oxford University Press, Oxford 1946.
'R.P.M.P.' W. G. Maclagan, 'Respect for Persons as a Moral Prin-
            ciple', *Philosophy* (1960).
T.M.S.   Adam Smith, *The Theory of Moral Sentiments*, in *British
            Moralists*, edited by L. A. Selby-Bigge, Bobbs-Merrill, New
            York 1964.

opening remark is that 'an ethic which finds the highest moral value in fellow-feeling, and attempts to derive all morally valuable conduct from this, cannot do justice to the facts of moral life' (p. 5). Now while I endorse this view, at the same time I want to point out that it is necessary to distinguish between the claim that all morally valuable conduct must be derived from sympathy, and the altogether different claim that sympathy as such, although not necessarily all the conduct it may inspire, is unconditionally morally valuable. I take the view that good reasons can be found for supporting the latter position. Kant's insistence on the autonomy of reason in ethics means that morality has to be conceived entirely in terms of respect for the moral law and that consequently any kind of sympathetic fellow-feeling must be at best morally neutral. But against this it can be argued that conscientiousness is in general merely a substitute for, among other things, sympathy, and that it might be possible to lead a genuinely moral life with sympathy at its focus and with only the minimum of recourse to any notion of duty. To maintain such a view certain questions must be faced. What is the extent to which it is appropriate to use moral language when talking about sympathetic feelings and sympathetic behaviour? For instance, does it make sense to say that people 'ought to be sympathetic'? If our feelings of sympathy are themselves both capricious and blind to value, is it still possible to attribute moral worth to experiencing such feelings? Furthermore, it can be claimed that the very capacity for moral discrimination logically presupposes a capacity for some kind of sympathetic feeling. Can a being unable to sympathize with others be said to possess true moral insight into his own and others' situations? In my final chapters I shall be exploring these crucial questions.

INTRODUCTION

THIS book attempts to clarify the principal philosophical connections between sympathy and morality. The concept of sympathy has figured prominently in the history of moral philosophy, and especially of British moral philosophy. There are two contexts in which it has appeared in particular. The first is in the 'altruism versus egoism' debate which occupied so much British moralists' time after Hobbes. I think I should make it clear from the outset that I intend to bypass this debate. My ultimate concern is with showing the extent to which the language of sympathy is in harmony with the language of moral discourse; and therefore any arguments to this end must remain untouched by whether or not one chooses to respond cynically to the suggestion that, as a fact about human behaviour, we are on occasion motivated by some kind of altruistic sympathy. Instead, we shall begin by looking at the second context in which the concept of sympathy has appeared—the question of the nature of moral judgement. Here, sympathy is thought to be important not for determining conduct but for evaluating conduct. This approach finds its classic exposition in David Hume's *Treatise of Human Nature*. I have chosen to devote a large proportion of my space to a fairly detailed study of the moral psychology of the *Treatise*, not only because of its intrinsic interest, but also because its central doctrine of sympathy as the 'medium' of moral judgement, as I shall call it, clearly illustrates what are, for ethics, the inherent limitations of sympathy: namely, its natural prejudice and its blindness to value. Separate chapters will discuss Hume's own concept of sympathy, the function of sympathy in the moral theory of the *Treatise*, the reasons for the unsatisfactoriness of this theory, and the relation between Hume's treatment of sympathy and that of Adam Smith in his major ethical work, *The Theory of Moral Sentiments*.

Rooted in moral sentimentalism (and, in Hume's case, associationist psychology), both these eighteenth-century sympathetic theories are basically unsatisfactory. But this does not mean that all the ethical possibilities of the concept of sympathy have been exhausted. In his book, *The Nature of Sympathy*, Max Scheler's

I

THE LOGIC OF SYMPATHY

THE purpose of this preliminary chapter is to provide the basic data with the help of which we can set about trying, first of all, to understand and evaluate Hume's sympathetic theory of moral judgement and, subsequently, to develop an account of the part the concept of sympathy plays in moral discourse. The immediate object is therefore the elucidation of the meaning of 'sympathy' and its grammatical derivatives 'sympathize', 'sympathetic', and 'sympathetically'. The concept is an extremely complicated one; the following examples illustrate the semantic range of 'sympathy' in one or other of its grammatical forms:

(a) The dockers struck in sympathy with the railway workers;
(b) He stopped to help out of sympathy;
(c) The Queen sent a message of sympathy to the bereaved families;
(d) The Home Secretary sympathized with those who wanted to bring back hanging but thought that a hasty decision would be unwise;
(e) He is known to sympathize with the Maoists;
(f) A murmur of anger ran sympathetically through the crowd;
(g) Palaeolithic man practised sympathetic magic;
(h) He made a sympathetic gesture.

Now whilst all the above uses of 'sympathy', 'sympathize', etc. are perfectly acceptable English, I have decided to isolate what appears to be the strongest (and incidentally, from an ethical point of view, the most interesting) sense and to limit the subsequent use of 'sympathy', 'sympathize', etc. to this particular sense only, unless otherwise indicated. There is an element of arbitrariness in doing this, but I think it is essential for the success of the whole discussion that we should have a clearly defined, purified concept of sympathy at our disposal. I particularly want to emphasize the vital distinction between the 'sympathy' which entails the idea of practical concern for another and the 'sympathy' which lacks or even precludes this idea and whose most convenient generic name would seem to be 'fellow-feeling'. The procedure I have decided to adopt in this chapter is first to set up a paradigm of

'sympathy' understood in its strongest sense. From this a tenta-
tive definition will emerge. I shall then consider some plausible
alternatives to this definition; during the process of which some
further implications of 'sympathy' will be teased out so that we
shall eventually be in a position to offer a more precise and relatively exhaustive definition of the word and to show in what
respects this differs from the weaker senses in which 'sympathy'
may be used. I should mention that, except in a few specific contexts (which I discuss), I have generally assumed there to be
a coincidence of meaning among the noun, verb, adjective, and
adverb.

The paradigm of 'sympathy' is this: A sympathizes 'with'
B 'about' some circumstances of B or 'in' some of B's feelings.
That is, the concept of sympathy is (a) interpersonal and (b)
intensional. I shall explain what I mean by these two terms.

(a) By saying that the concept of sympathy is 'interpersonal'
I mean that it can only hold between or among persons. We can
only predicate '. . . sympathizes' of a person. But this sympathetic
agent cannot just sympathize: he must sympathize 'with another'.
This other must be, or be believed by the agent to be, a sentient
being—a being which can feel and suffer, be helped and be
harmed. In this context I take 'person' to be equivalent to 'sentient
being' because it does not seem to be a condition that the 'other'
should be able to understand what it is to sympathize. We can
sympathize with infants and idiots; and I do not think that it is
stretching a point to suggest that we can sympathize with the
bull in the ring or the rabbit in the trap. 'Sympathy' has regard for
'the other' solely in respect of his capacity to feel and to suffer.
Differences based on class, race, nationality, religion, culture, possessions, education, character, intelligence, taste, and all the other
grounds which have been found for discriminating against people,
are all pushed equally into the background. It is true that in practice sympathy is partial. For instance, we are more likely to sympathize with someone of whom we approve and less likely with
someone of whom we disapprove; so much so that in the minds
of some to say that you sympathize with another person is almost
tantamount to saying that you recommend that person's character
and conduct. But the point is that sympathy is not necessarily
influenced in such a way. I may happen to find a person's conduct,
character, and whole style of life utterly repellent; but this does
not rule out the possibility of my sympathizing with him. I may

have no wish to emulate Genet or Christie but I can nevertheless sympathize with them. Although what a man does and what he is like may be made into psychological obstacles to sympathy, they can never be made into logical obstacles. As for the sympathetic agent himself, it is clear that he must be a *thinking* as well as a feeling creature; for he must possess the capacities for self-consciousness and imagination. In general, then, it would seem that where it is true to say that A sympathizes with B it must follow that A is a thinking and feeling being and B at the very least a feeling being.

(b) But not only do we sympathize 'with another', we also sympathize 'about something' or 'in something'. However, there are formal restrictions on what this object may be; it is limited to the range of what can be or be believed to be (i) the other's circumstances or state of mind and (ii) unpleasant in some way or other. On being told that A sympathizes with B it is always sensible to ask what it is that A is sympathizing 'about'. An appropriate answer to such a question would consist in mentioning a particular set of circumstances. This set of circumstances would have to bear some connection with B. It is impossible for A to sympathize with B about C's misfortunes unless these in some way affect B. Thus if C fails his examinations A cannot sympathize with B about this unless B were, say, C's teacher or parent. The circumstances about which we sympathize with others are always unpleasant and involve some kind of suffering: it would sound odd to say that one sympathized with a person who was enjoying himself or having a good time. Examples of the sort of things we sympathize with people about are bereavements, estrangements, failures, ill health, and bad luck. But it would make equally good sense on being informed that A sympathizes with B to ask what it is that A is sympathizing with B 'in'. And an appropriate answer to this question would consist in mentioning some feeling (in the loosest sense of the word) which we think A is experiencing. We sympathize with others 'in' their grief, anxiety, frustration, disappointment, humiliation, and so on. It follows, therefore, that it is *both* the other person's state of mind *and* his circumstances which are to be regarded as the objects of the sympathy. The logical situation is not properly described by saying that we sympathize with another *either* about his circumstances *or* in his feelings *or* sometimes both about his circumstances and in his feelings. The point is that whether one is referring to the circumstances or the feelings one is still referring to the same *state of affairs*. The state of affairs is not just the bereavement or the grief but the *grief at the bereavement*, not just the precariousness of the employment or the anxiety but the *anxiety over the precariousness of the employment*. Feelings are logically connected to the circumstances in which they are experienced; and the particular circumstances in which another person is placed are one of the criteria we use for deciding what is his state of mind. The grief and the bereavement, the anxiety and the precariousness, are not contingently but logically connected to each other; and they must be thought of as making up together the states of affairs which are the logically proper objects of 'sympathy'.

It is useful to consider in this context the notions of misplaced and misguided sympathy. Sympathy is *misplaced* when the agent makes a mistake as to the other's state of mind. Often it is a question of believing that another is in some kind of distress and needing help when he is not. I might have thought that someone was frightened when in fact he was only pretending to be frightened or when he was in fact angry. This kind of error typically arises through not taking into full account the other's behaviour or his character, not looking beyond the immediate circumstances in which he is placed, relying too heavily on what one's *own* reaction to such a situation would be and so forth. In short, sympathy is misplaced when the agent misjudges the true state of affairs. On the other hand, if sympathy is *misguided* then a mistake has been made in a different area. For sympathy is misguided when the agent has failed to realize the most appropriate way of *helping* the other person. One safeguard at least that the help we offer is the right sort of help is that we should have considered the other person's own wishes, whether they are articulated verbally or expressed less directly. The blind man may not want to be fussed over—and to do so would be to show a lack of understanding of his predicament, a lack of imagination. True, it is not always easy to know what to do for the best; for example, the blind man may want no help at all, however discreetly it is offered. I do not want to suggest that the sympathetic action is necessarily the one which coincides with the other's wishes— for it is a truism that we do not always know what is for our own good and that even if we do we do not always desire it—but that the sympathetic agent, if he wants to minimize the risk of acting in the wrong way, always takes account of the other's wishes even if he does not carry them out. I may sympathize sincerely with another but feel bound to cause him suffering in the interests of what I judge to be his own long-term benefit. Moreover, it is quite possible for me to sympathize with someone without his being aware of it. In some cases sympathy may merely lead me to omit certain actions I should otherwise have carried out but which through sympathy I have recognized would cause harm to another person. We can be sympathetic without 'showing' sympathy; that is, without performing overtly sympathetic actions like commiserating, consoling, comforting, and congratulating. With some individuals and in some situations to 'show' one's sympathy in such a manner is not the best way of being sympathetic. In such cases we have tried to tread the delicate line between being irritatingly over-solicitous and appearing to be coldly indifferent.[1]

In the light of the above discussion I want to propose tentatively the following definition of the meaning of 'sympathy'. On the face of the matter, it seems reasonable to argue that if it can be truly said that A sympathizes with B it must be at least the case that (a) there is fellow-feeling, and (b) A is concerned for B's welfare. I shall discuss each of these requirements in turn.

Fellow-Feeling: Most kinds of sympathy seem to entail a sharing of emotions which I have called 'fellow-feeling'. The trouble is that 'fellow-feeling' is an over-worked and consequently ambiguous term. When faced with the problem of clarifying it the immediate temptation may be to say that it is equivalent to 'having the same feeling as another person'. I think this move brings

---

[1] There is another case which is often instanced, misleadingly, as 'misguided' sympathy. Suppose a habitual fare-dodger has ended up in court. Now some people might say that he has been asking for trouble and that because of this if we sympathize with him we are wasting our sympathy upon him. By his behaviour he has *forfeited his right* to the sympathy of others: if we are sympathetically disposed towards him our sympathy is 'misguided'. But this kind of situation is significantly different from the typical case of 'misguided' sympathy already discussed. 'Misguided' sympathy characteristically involves a certain kind of mistake on the agent's part. His realization of this mistake must affect what he can sensibly say about his attitude towards the other person: if he discovers that the other man is not after all suffering in any way then he cannot sensibly continue asserting that he is 'sympathetic' towards him. But, on the contrary, although I may discover that the man with whom I sympathize has asked for the trouble he is in, and further, although I may recognize in this that he has forfeited his right to my sympathy, I can (although I may not want to) continue to assert that I 'sympathize' with him. In this kind of case, then, no mistake need have been made by the agent and even if one has been made its discovery need not affect the agent's sympathy.

several difficulties. To begin with, since we can only experience
our own feelings, strictly speaking it must be impossible 'to have
the same feeling as another'. If we were to experience another's
feelings we should have to be identical with that person; and it is
impossible to be more than one person at a time. Furthermore,
even if we substitute 'a similar' for 'the same' it seems to follow
that I cannot have fellow-feeling with another who is, say, suffering unless I suffer similarly. Now although there are certain kinds
of situation (see pp. 12–17) where it could be reasonably argued
both that fellow-feeling is present and that the agent is 'having
feelings similar to another's' these cases are far from typical. In
the typical case of fellow-feeling, where A has fellow-feeling
with B who is suffering, to insist that A must be suffering himself
would be very peculiar. Not only would this misrepresent the
nature of fellow-feeling in its most common context, it would
also be very difficult to see how a person could be sensibly said
to be suffering although not in any circumstances which explain
that suffering.

It is worth noting, though, that the first-person use of 'to have
fellow-feeling with another' does not function in the way that one
would perhaps expect of a first-person psychological statement.
In the *Investigations* (i, section 244, and ii. ix, sections 187–9)
Wittgenstein has drawn attention to the fact that, amongst a
diversity of functions, such statements are used to express
emotions—thus the words 'I am afraid' have certain features in
common with a cry of fear. But it is clear that 'I have fellow-
feeling with John' does not typically function so as to express an
emotion in this way at all. Rather, such an utterance would seem
to consist of, at least in part, a claim to have some kind of *knowledge* about John's state of mind. This means that fellow-feeling,
in so far as it is entailed by sympathy, is characterized by a *cognitive* element. Since I do not think that we can simply identify
fellow-feeling with knowledge of another's state of mind, the
question arises as to what is the difference between the two. It has
been suggested (Leslie Stephen, *Science of Ethics*, p. 221) that in
order to know what another is feeling we have to have fellow-
feeling with him. I would disagree with this. With some exceptions (to be discussed later), it does not seem that there can be
fellow-feeling without knowledge; whereas there can be knowledge without fellow-feeling. It is not in the least contradictory
to say that I know what another is feeling but that I do not share

his feeling. Where fellow-feeling differs from merely knowing that another has a certain feeling is in its *affective* element. This affection is characteristically *imaginative*. Fellow-feeling is an exercise of the imagination in that it involves an imaginative representation of another's feelings. In order to achieve this we have to feel ourselves into the other's situation. We have to imagine *what it is to be him*. It is essential that we go beyond merely putting ourselves in his situation. It is a common mistake amongst writers on the subject to suppose that fellow-feeling or sympathy in so far as it entails fellow-feeling consists in imagining what one would feel if one were in the other person's place. For instance, Alexander Bain suggests that sympathy or compassion is 'the vicarious position' and consists in 'making the other's case [one's] own' (*The Emotions and the Will*, p. 113). H. B. Acton suggests that if a person is to pity another then he 'must imagine himself as suffering similarly' ('E.I.S.', p. 66). And as we shall later see in Chapter V the same idea occurs in Adam Smith's *The Theory of Moral Sentiments*. But it is not enough that I should imagine how *I* should feel if *I* were in the other person's place; I have to imagine how *he* feels, having the temperament and personality that *he* has. This imaginative realization of another's feelings entails, but is quite distinct from, the knowledge or belief that this person has certain feelings.

In order to have fellow-feeling with another is it necessary, we may ask, that we should have been previously in a similar situation and felt feelings similar to those of the other person? For instance, is it logically possible for someone who has never been in prison to share the feelings of someone who is in prison? Or is it sufficient that he should have experienced analogous situations and feelings? The answer to this seems to be that I cannot have fellow-feeling, or therefore sympathize, with someone who is, say, in pain or anxious if I do not know what it is to feel pain or to be anxious. If it so happened that I were pathologically incapable of feeling pain then presumably I should never be able to learn the meaning of the word 'pain'. Possibly I could be taught to use the word on the appropriate occasions; but even so it would only be *as if* I knew the meaning of the word and I should be parasitic on my instructor. If this were the case then I could never be truly said to have fellow-feeling or sympathize with someone who was in pain. But once I have grasped the full meaning of the word 'pain' then I can sympathize with those who are in pain even though I may never have experienced (and never shall) the particular kind of pain they are experiencing. As a man I can sympathize with a woman in childbirth; and I can sympathize with someone with toothache even though I may never have had toothache. To say this, though, is not to deny the psychological fact that those who are emotionally inexperienced are not so well-equipped as they might be to share the sufferings of other people. The good novelist, for instance, must feel at home in those areas of human psychology he chooses to investigate—Jane Austen might not have fared so well in Hemingway territory and vice versa.

The concept of cognitive fellow-feeling discussed above is only one species of fellow-feeling and I shall shortly be considering what other kinds may exist and their connection with the concept of sympathy. Before I leave this section what I want to emphasize once more is that it is the concept of *cognitive* fellow-feeling which is logically fundamental to that of sympathy. In this sense 'fellow-feeling' must be understood not as an instinctive tuning-in to another's emotional state but rather as an exercise involving both the capacity for self-consciousness and the capacity for imagination.

Concern: Where cognitive fellow-feeling is to be distinguished from sympathy is in the fact that the former does not entail the active concern for others which the latter concept does. In fellow-feeling there is no *conative* element. But, on the contrary, when we sympathize with another who is suffering then not only do we imaginatively participate in this suffering but we are also disposed to do something about it: we cannot sympathize with someone and yet remain indifferent to him. With this in mind, Schweitzer has drawn attention to what he takes to be the paradoxical nature of Indian religious teaching:

Indian religion likes to represent itself as the religion of universal sympathy. It talks a good deal about the compassion we should feel for all creatures. At the same time, however, it preaches the ideal of being absolutely without interest and of ceasing from all activity and maintains that even the enthusiasm for doing good must be considered as a passion which in the end has to be overcome. From intellectual compassion the Brahmanist and the Buddhist do not advance to the compassion of deed. (*Christianity and the Religions of the World*, p. 48)

It is contradictory to assert both that we sympathize with another and that we are not benevolently disposed towards him at least in respect of his capacity to feel and to suffer. It follows that the notion of 'intellectual compassion' is self-contradictory. Sympathy is inescapably a *practical* concept. It is important to note that we do not necessarily have actually to do anything in order to be justified in claiming that we sympathize with another. As I have already mentioned, sympathy may lead us to omit certain actions which would, if performed, hurt the other person. Moreover, there are some occasions on which we are justified in not helping the person with whom we sympathize; for instance, where the performance of the sympathetic action would be incompatible with the fulfilment of a promise or the execution of the law. However, it would appear to be a rare situation where we could not *in some way* help the person with whom we sympathize. In a case where A asserts that he sympathizes with B but subsequently, though it is within his power to do so, does nothing aimed at alleviating B's plight, we should be justified, unless A could produce reasonable grounds for his inaction, in concluding that he was either lying or weak-willed or misusing the word 'sympathy'.

Notice that this 'concern' for another which is entailed by 'sympathy' is altruistic or disinterested. It is very possible that my concern for the welfare of another is based on purely selfish motives. I may be concerned for another's health, his safety, his comfort—not for his own sake—but because I desire to be well-thought-of or because I have a guilty conscience or because I want to get him into my debt. Sympathy is just one among many possible motives for wanting to help another person. But the help which is offered out of sympathy is without interest: there can be no ulterior motive for sympathetic concern.

I now want to move on to discuss some alternative suggestions for a definition of the meaning of 'sympathy'. On the basis of ordinary language I think we could suggest that in one context or another 'sympathy' is used as equivalent in meaning to the following:

(1) 'fellow-feeling';
(2) 'knowing what another is feeling';
(3) 'being in agreement with another's opinion'; and
(4) 'feeling sorry for another' or 'pity'.

I shall try to show in what respects each of these equivalents differs from the definition I have already outlined, namely that 'sympathy' entails 'fellow-feeling' together with 'concern'. What follows should help towards sharpening this preliminary definition.

1. *'Fellow-feeling'*

This can be divided into *cognitive* and *non-cognitive*; the discussion has so far centred around the first of these. Now where these two concepts differ from each other is in respect of the agent's awareness of the subjectivity of the other, of the existence of another centre of consciousness. While it is a necessary (though not sufficient) condition for there to be cognitive fellow-feeling that such awareness should exist, its existence is neither a necessary nor a sufficient condition for non-cognitive fellow-feeling. Enough has already been said to show that the concept of 'cognitive fellow-feeling', although entailed by 'sympathy', cannot be held to be identical with 'sympathy'. Furthermore, it could be argued that cognitive fellow-feeling is perfectly compatible with hatred and cruelty. For does not the delight in the suffering of others in which cruelty consists depend to a great extent on the capacity to realize these sufferings in the imagination? Considered in itself, cognitive fellow-feeling is passive; and because of this it is compatible with both a benevolent and a malevolent interest in the other person.

But non-cognitive fellow-feeling, although not excluding the psychological possibility of practical sympathy, can never be the logical ground for this sympathy. By 'non-cognitive fellow-feeling' I mean to include such concepts as emotional infection, emotional identification, and 'community of feeling'. Of these, in at least emotional infection and 'community of feeling' it is true to say that one person, rather than imagining another's mental state, actually does experience feelings very close to that other person's. If, as I suggest, in this kind of fellow-feeling the agent is *not* aware of the subjectivity of the other, then the possibility of the practical concern which is necessary to sympathy is ruled out. If 'sympathizing' were equivalent in meaning to 'having fellow-feeling with another' then it would be correct to talk about 'sympathizing' both in the case of imaginative fellow-feeling and in the cases of emotional infection, identification, and 'community of feeling'. But not only is it the case that 'fellow-feeling'—cognitive and non-cognitive—is not identical in meaning with 'sympathy', but it is also the case, as I shall shortly show in more detail, that each of the last-named concepts and that of sympathy are independent of each other. That A is infected by B, that A emotionally identifies himself with B, and that there is a 'community of feeling' between A and B are all logically unconnected with A's sympathy for B.

Emotional Infection or Contagion: This is sometimes referred to as 'animal sympathy'. It is particularly manifest in herds or groups of gregarious animals. It is just as apparent in a football crowd as in a flock of sheep. When A has been infected by B then what, on the face of it, has happened is that a particular feeling initially felt only by B has somehow been transferred to A with the result that he can be said to be experiencing a feeling similar to B's. We all have the tendency to adopt, or at least be affected by, the mood of our immediate neighbours. When we demand to have cheerful faces about us or go to a party with the express intention of being 'taken out of ourselves', the hope is that we shall become infected by the prevailing atmosphere. That there is such a phenomenon as emotional infection is a fundamental assumption in the study of the psychology of the crowd and the psychology of individuals when they form groups and act in concert. Le Bon supposed that the crowd possesses a corporate personality somehow distinct from those of its individual members. At political demonstrations, mass rallies, and football matches individuals may find it very difficult to resist being caught up in the mass emotion or group of emotions. In such situations the dominant feeling is self-propagating, the words, gestures, and actions of each individual being reflected and magnified again and again in those of his neighbours. When we find ourselves in a group we behave rather differently from how we should when with one other person or by ourselves. The boundaries of individuality may become so blurred and the notion of personal responsibility so diminished that acts of the most appalling inhumanity and, but less frequently, of the noblest self-sacrifice may be performed. Intoxication by such mass emotions as racial hatred, religious enthusiasm, and pop hysteria all depend on this innate susceptibility to infection.

Where there is infection, then, it is correct to say that two or more individuals are experiencing similar feelings; and for this reason infection is to be considered as a kind of fellow-feeling. Where it differs, though, from the cognitive fellow-feeling of practical sympathy is that it does not imply an awareness in the agent of the true subject of the emotion, a knowledge that the emotion 'really belongs to' another person. One might say that the emotion that the infected person is feeling is just as 'real' for

him as it is for the person who infected him in the first place. The
emotion in question is not realized in the imagination of the
agent, as it is in cognitive fellow-feeling. It is possible to become
as cheerful or as angry as our companions without knowing *why*
they are cheerful or angry or even *that* they are cheerful or angry.
Although the mob's anger has to have an object, and finds it in
a scapegoat, this object does not have to be deserving of anger so
long as the mob believes it to be. In short, infection does not presuppose a capacity for self-consciousness in those who are infected.

If it is possible for me to be infected by another without realizing it, it follows that in infection I need not be aware of the
existence of this other as a feeling subject whom it is within my
power to help or harm. This is reflected in the locution 'to sympathize with anger, fear, excitement . . .' (cf. the paradigm of
'sympathy' in its strongest sense at the beginning of the chapter).
When we say that we sympathize with a feeling without any
reference to the person whose feeling it is, then it is very likely
that we are using 'sympathy' as equivalent to 'infection'. If in
infection there is a sense in which I am aware of another person's
existence then this is merely as a *cause* of my present feelings—not
as a sentient being in his own right. Thus I may shun contact with
those who are suffering horribly on account of the distasteful or
distressing feelings which are communicated to me by their
presence. In such a case I am interested in these others only in so
far as they are causes of my own uneasiness.

It should be clear that the transference of feeling from one
person to another which is infection is quite distinct from the
imaginative realization of another's feelings which is cognitive
fellow-feeling. 'Sympathy' entails a practical concern for another.
Such concern requires a prior recognition of the other's existence
as a centre of consciousness. But this recognition is not entailed
by 'emotional infection'.

Emotional Identification: If *A* emotionally identifies himself with
B then he is necessarily unaware of his individual identity as distinct from that of *B*. It is only to an observer that it makes sense
to say that there is fellow-feeling; for *A* himself is unaware of the
vicariousness of what he is feeling. If one person immerses himself in the personality of another then it must be impossible to
talk of the one being concerned for the other. In order to help
clarify what is a very problematic concept we can turn to Scheler

who, in *The Nature of Sympathy*, deals at some length with the phenomenon and gives many interesting illustrations. He cites the identification of each member of a totem with an individual member of the totem species:

According to Von den Steinen, the Boroso allege that they are really identical with red parrots (araras), each member of the totem with a particular red parrot. It is not just that the destiny (birth, sickness, death) of the member of the totem is mysteriously linked with that of his totem animal in a merely causal sense; this connexion is really no more than a consequence of their actual *identity*. . . . The literal identification of a man with his ancestors is another case in point: he is not merely like his ancestor, or guided and ruled by him, but actually *is*, in his present life, at the same time one of his ancestors. This stage of historical identification between man and his ancestor is prior to anything implied by the term 'ancestor-cult'. This cult and its emotional bond with the ancestor in the form of piety, ritual obligation, etc., already represents a first stage of *liberation* from the primitive identification of the descendant with his ancestor, and presupposes a recognition that the two are distinct individuals. (*N.S.*, p. 19.)

and the identification of the hypnotist and his subject:

Genuine identification is also present where the relationship between the hypnotist and his subject is not just a temporary one, in which particular acts and undertakings are suggested, but becomes a stable and permanent state, such that the hypnotic subject is continuously 'wrapped up' in all the individual personal attitudes of the hypnotist, thinks only his thoughts, wills only with his will, esteems his values, loves with his loves and hates with his hate—but at the same time is convinced that this other self with all its attitudes and forms of action is really his own. But whereas in primitive identification we have a genuine identification of *existence*, in intensified suggestion through continuous hypnosis, involving not merely specific acts and performances, but an adoption of the whole concrete outlook of the hypnotist, we have only an identification of *character*, coupled with an awareness of separation in actual existence. (*N.S.*, p. 20.)

Scheler also mentions sadism, masochism, the crowd's identification with its leader, and the child's identification with its mother in this context. To these you can add the aesthetic experience (often known as 'empathy') of an audience's identification with a particular character in a film, book, or play. What all these examples involve is a total submergence of one person's consciousness in another's. The Boroso do not recognize themselves as distinct from the red parrots; the hypnotist's patient does not think of his feelings as 'really belonging to' the hypnotist; and when we watch *King Lear* there will be at least certain moments when we *are* King Lear. It is clear, then, that although emotional identification is a kind of fellow-feeling it is not the kind which is the basis of sympathy. Logically prior to my concern for another is my recognition of his existence as a being separate from myself. The notions of concern for another and emotional identification are mutually exclusive. Rousseau was at best mis-leading when he analysed 'compassion' in terms of identification: 'Compassion must, in fact, be the stronger, the more the animal beholding any kind of distress identifies himself with the animal which suffers.' (*Origin of Inequality*, p. 199.) For the more perfectly I identify myself with another the less sense there is in supposing that I can be disposed to help him. What perhaps Rousseau should have said was that compassion was the stronger the more fully we identify ourselves with the other *in our imaginations*. For this would not rule out our awareness of the distinction between our-self and the other.

Community of Feeling: This is Scheler's expression. There is a sense in which two people may be said to be feeling the same feeling without any prior communication of any sort from the one to the other. Scheler gives the following example:

> Two parents stand beside the body of a beloved child. They feel in common the 'same' sorrow, the 'same' anguish. It is not that *A* feels this sorrow and *B* feels it also, and moreover that they both know that they are feeling it. No, it is a *feeling-in-common*. *A*'s sorrow is in no way an 'external' matter for *B* here, as it is, e.g. for their friend *C*, who joins them, and commiserates 'with them' or 'upon their sorrow'. (*N.S.*, p. 12.)

Leaving aside the question whether there is any more in the notion of 'feeling-in-common' than there is in the notion of 'having feelings similar to another's', it is, I think reasonable to regard Scheler's example as an instance of a kind of fellow-feeling which is distinct from those mentioned so far. But again we can dis-tinguish it from the fellow-feeling which 'sympathy' entails. Whilst it is perhaps possible to say that the two parents are 'in sympathy', this is certainly not the same as saying that either 'sympathizes' with the other. For there is a good sense in which their feelings are their own—as opposed to being experienced through their imaginations. The origin of each of their sets of feelings is independent of that of the other. We may say that their feelings are 'in sympathy' in so far as they harmonize; but the fact that the feelings of two individuals happen to harmonize in this fashion does not imply that they have to be aware of each other's existence as feeling subjects.

At this stage I hope that I have succeeded in showing (a) that 'sympathy' can never be simply equated with 'fellow-feeling' and (b) that the fellow-feeling upon which sympathy is conceptually dependent is exclusively what I have termed *cognitive* fellow-feeling. The vital feature which is absent from all *non*-cognitive fellow-feeling is the agent's awareness of both himself and the other person; and without this awareness the possibility of active sympathy is precluded. Of course, I do not mean to suggest that it is not psychologically possible for, say, an instance of infection to be followed by an attitude of practical concern for another person (including even that person who is the source of the infection); but only that infection (together with emotional identification, community of feeling, and any other kind of non-cognitive fellow-feeling which I may have omitted to mention) is logically independent of such practical sympathy.

2. *'Knowing Another's Feelings'*

Now I think that sometimes when we say that we sympathize with another person we are in effect asserting no more than that we know how he is feeling—that is, we do not feel that we are committing ourselves actually to helping him. This is especially clear if we consider the implications of the sentence 'I can sympathize with you' as it is often used. On the contrary, I should want to maintain that whilst there is nothing self-contradictory about 'I know that you're feeling very miserable but I don't sympathize with you' there is something distinctly self-contradictory about the sentence 'I sympathize with you but I don't want to help you'. Knowledge of the state of another's mind is a necessary but not a sufficient condition of sympathy with that person. The callous man knows full well that another person is suffering but he refuses to realize the other person's experience in his own imagination and is consequently indifferent to it. By contrast the stupid or insensitive man is not even aware that anyone else is suffering.

3. 'Agreement'

'Sympathy' can be equivalent in meaning to 'being in total or partial agreement'. In this sense we can sympathize with the attitudes, opinions, beliefs, aims, ideals, and policies not only of individuals but also of such bodies as committees, political parties, town councils, trade unions, and governments. In particular we talk of sympathizing with political parties, groups, factions, and movements. The difference between, for instance, a Maoist and a Maoist sympathizer largely amounts to a question of their respective degrees of committal to Maoist doctrines: either because of some theoretical reservation or out of prudence or fear the sympathizer prefers not to commit himself openly and wholeheartedly to Maoism. Very often there is an explicit or implicit 'but'; as in, for example, 'The Home Secretary sympathizes with those who want to reintroduce the death penalty but thinks that a hasty decision would be unwise.' Although we can see that other person's point of view and to some extent go along with it, we nevertheless cannot wholeheartedly accept it. This metaphorical use of 'sympathy' is analogous to the use of 'feel' in such sentences as 'I feel that to devalue would be the best policy.' When we ask people what they 'feel' about a matter we are only asking for their opinions—not for statements about their emotions. Once we have realized the metaphorical nature of the language, the many and varied contexts in which it is appropriate to use the term 'sympathy' should not present any anomalies.

4. 'Pity' and 'Feeling Sorry'

It is important to distinguish 'sympathy' from 'pity' and 'feeling sorry for'. The use of the word 'pity' in a particular context seems to imply that the speaker is in some way better off than the person who is pitied. The king pities the subject; the judge pities the prisoner; the sane man pities the idiot; mankind pities the beasts. We implore others 'to have pity on us' in much the same way as we implore tham 'to have mercy on us'. 'I pity you' is more often than not equivalent to 'I despise you'. It does not even appear that 'pity' entails an attitude of concern towards the other creature —although, of course, it is often used as an explanation for helping. In similar fashion, to say that we 'feel sorry for' someone may also be an expression of our contempt for him. The semantic gap between 'sympathy' and 'feeling sorry for' is an even greater gap than that between 'sympathy' and 'pity'. 'Sympathy is a good start,' reads the Oxfam advertisement, 'but when you read about the sickening poverty on the other half of the world, feeling sorry isn't quite enough.' In equating 'sympathy' with 'feeling sorry' the copywriter has made an error. It might occur to me as I eat my pork chop to say that I 'felt sorry' for the pig, but it would be odd or whimsical to say that I 'sympathized' with the animal. Maybe this is because there is by then no question of my helping the animal. In any case it is certainly the case that 'feeling sorry for' lacks the conative element that characterizes 'sympathy': if I 'feel sorry' for someone I may be disposed to help him but I need not be. The contexts in which it is appropriate to use 'feeling sorry' merge easily into those where the use of 'regret' would be appropriate.

'Sympathy' differs from 'pity' and 'feeling sorry', then, in two important respects. The first is that 'pity' and 'feeling sorry' do not necessarily imply a concern for the welfare of the other person. The second is that they both nearly always carry with them overtones of condescension which, although not necessarily absent from all uses of 'sympathy' (consider 'I don't want your sympathy!'), is certainly not a typical connotation of 'sympathy'.

We are now in a position to expand our initial definition of the meaning of 'sympathy'. I want to maintain that if it is correct to make the statement 'A sympathizes with B' then the following conditions must be fulfilled:
(a) A is aware of the existence of B as a sentient subject;
(b) A knows or believes he knows B's state of mind;
(c) there is fellow-feeling between A and B so that through his imagination A is able to realize B's state of mind; and
(d) A is altruistically concerned for B's welfare.
Each of the above conditions is a necessary, though not sufficient, condition of the truth of the statement 'A sympathizes with B' when 'sympathizes' is understood in its strongest sense.[1] It should now be clear how this practical sympathy, although entailing cognitive fellow-feeling, must itself be sharply separated from all other kinds of fellow-feeling, both cognitive and non-cognitive.

This distinction is vital for a clear understanding of Hume's concept of sympathy in the *Treatise*.

---

[1] It could be argued that not all the conditions I have mentioned here are of the same logical status; particularly that some are logically prior to others. But to go into this question would be lengthy and of no especial service to my main theme.

II

HUME'S CONCEPT OF SYMPATHY

OF the topics discussed by Hume in the—until recently[1]—relatively neglected Book Two of the *Treatise of Human Nature*,[2] sympathy is the most important. The moral philosophy of Book Three cannot be properly understood without reference to the philosophy of mind, especially the doctrine of sympathy, which is contained in the second Book—entitled 'Of the Passions'. According to Book Three, moral judgement is the function of the disinterested spectator. When we call someone's conduct or character (including our own) 'virtuous' or 'vicious' then we mean that we have contemplated it from an impartial point of view and that we have experienced a feeling of either approval or disapproval towards it. Approval consists of a special feeling of pleasure or satisfaction and disapproval of a special feeling of pain, uneasiness, or disgust. These latter feelings are essentially of a sympathetic origin and result from the spectator's sympathy both with the feelings of the person whose conduct and character he is appraising and with the feelings of those who are affected by this conduct. Hume makes moral evaluation ultimately dependent on this sympathetic communication of feeling. In the next chapter I shall discuss in some detail this theory of sympathy as the medium of moral judgement; but before this I want to try to ascertain, as far as possible without reference to the specifically ethical parts of the *Treatise*, exactly what Hume has in mind when he writes the word 'sympathy'.

The first thing that strikes one is that despite the great importance Hume attaches to sympathy in the *Treatise* nowhere in this work can be found what could be called a definition of 'sympathy'. His account of the genesis of sympathy (*Treatise*, pp. 316–24) is the closest he gets to giving the reader a definition. It seems

---

[1] Páll S. Árdal's *Passion and Value in Hume's Treatise* (Edinburgh, 1966) convincingly emphasizes the positive relationship between Hume's ethics and his philosophy of mind as expressed in Book Two.

[2] Books One ('Of the Understanding') and Two ('Of the Passions') were first published in 1739, Book Three ('Of Morals') in 1740. All references will be to the Selby-Bigge edition (Clarendon Press, Oxford).

reasonable to adopt this account as Hume's model of sympathy and to try to extract from it a definition of 'sympathy'. I shall argue that most of the time Hume sees sympathy as a kind of emotional infection and that in consequence of this he fails to leave room for the practical concern for the other which in the previous chapter was emphasized as an essential part of the meaning of 'sympathy' understood in its strongest sense. However, in a later section of Book Two (*Treatise*, pp. 381–9) Hume does make some attempt to connect sympathy and practice. But this attempt is vitiated, it seems to me, through Hume's inability to distinguish clearly between a psychological explanation and a logical one. What is ostensibly a causal account of the connection between sympathy and practical benevolence turns out to beg the question. It is possible to understand the 'extensive sympathy' to which Hume appeals in the course of this explanation as implying a broadening of the meaning of 'sympathy' from that of mere infection to something more practical. But it is difficult to find a consistent interpretation of what Hume means by 'extensive sympathy'. In any case, any interpretation of 'sympathy' as involving practical concern is ultimately bound to be undermined by Hume's fundamental conception of all fellow-feeling as non-cognitive rather than cognitive. The extent to which Hume's concept of sympathy is restricted and these criticisms justified will become plainer as we progress.

Hume thinks of sympathy primarily as the transference or communication of an emotion, sensation, or even an opinion from one individual to another:

No quality of human nature is more remarkable, both in itself and in its consequences, than that propensity we have to sympathize with others, and to receive by communication their inclinations and sentiments, however different from, or even contrary to our own. (*Treatise*, p. 316.)

According to this account, then, sympathy is emphatically *not* a passion or emotion of any kind.[1] Exactly how this communication of emotion takes place is described in very mechanical terms in the account of the genesis of sympathy. But before discussing this account we should say something about the underlying picture of the emotions that seems to be implied.

---

[1] D. G. C. MacNabb suggests at least once that sympathy *is* a passion (*David Hume: his Theory of Knowledge and Morality*, p. 166).

Hume's initial classification of the passions, to be found in the introduction to Book Two, is, despite its prominence, a somewhat misleading statement of his views. The basic assumption from which Hume starts is that all perceptions are either ideas or impressions. Ideas are weak copies of impressions and differ from them only in vivacity. The impressions may be divided into (a) *original* and (b) *secondary* or *reflective*. The original impressions are natural instincts or impulses not founded on any precedent perception of pleasure or pain; that is, they are impressions of the senses and all bodily pains and pleasures. On the other hand, the secondary or reflective impressions are founded on or aroused in and through precedent impressions of pain and pleasure. What distinguishes the original from the secondary impressions, then, is that whilst the original arise without any preceding thought or perception, the immediate occasion of a secondary impression's being experienced is some antecedent perception of pleasure or pain. Now why this section is misleading is because from what Hume goes on to say (*Treatise*, p. 276) the reader might be led to believe that the secondary impressions are divided into the calm and violent passions and that in turn the violent are subdivided into the direct and indirect passions. In fact, though, from later statements it is clear that the violent/calm classification is a dichotomy which cuts straight across the direct/indirect classification. The calmness or violence of a passion refers to the *intensity* with which the passion is felt rather than to its mode of origin.[1] Hume admits that the division is not very exact and that what is normally a violent passion may on occasion 'decay into so soft an emotion, as to become, in a manner, imperceptible' (*Treatise*, p. 276) and that what is normally a calm emotion may in similar fashion come to be felt with great intensity. Properly speaking, we should call the violent impressions 'passions' and the calm ones 'emotions'. The sense of beauty and deformity is mentioned as a calm passion; love and hatred, pride and humility, grief and joy, as violent passions. Therefore the violence of a passion must be distinguished from its strength. The strength of a passion refers to its motivating force; and thus a passion can be both calm and strong: '. . . when a passion has once become a settled principle of action, and is the predominant inclination of the soul, it commonly produces no longer any sensible agitation.' (*Treatise*,

---

[1] My interpretation of the calm passions has been influenced by Árdal's chapter on the topic (op. cit., pp. 93–108).

pp. 418–19.) By contrast, the direct/indirect classification of passions refers to the origins of the passions: 'By direct passions I understand such as arise immediately from good or evil, from pain or pleasure. By indirect such as proceed from the same principles, but by the conjunction of other qualities.' (*Treatise*, p. 276.) The direct passions, such as desire, aversion, grief, joy, hope, fear, despair, and security, are aroused immediately by feelings of pleasure or pain or by the thought of these feelings. The indirect passions, such as pride and humility, love and hatred, ambition and vanity, pity and malice, are aroused by the same things but with the conjunction of other qualities. But Hume does not seem to adhere to this division very strictly. Later (*Treatise*, p. 439) he cites as direct passions 'the desire of punishment to our enemies, and of happiness to our friends; hunger, lust, and a few other bodily appetites', saying that these passions produce pleasure and pain rather than proceed from such feelings. Moreover, elsewhere (*Treatise*, p. 417) Hume mentions benevolence, resentment, love of life and kindness to children as examples of 'instincts originally implanted in our natures'. Since none of the passions mentioned in these two contexts are said to arise from precedent perceptions of pleasure or pain they cannot be what Hume means by 'secondary' impressions. At the same time (apart from hunger and lust) they are distinct from bodily impressions and cannot be thought of as 'original' impressions. Kemp Smith conveniently lumps them together and calls them the 'primary' passions (*The Philosophy of David Hume*, p. 168).

It is to the study of the origins of the indirect passions, in particular love, hatred, pride, and humility, that Hume devotes most of Book Two of the *Treatise*. He distinguishes between the *cause* of an indirect passion, its *sensation*, and its *object*. Now Hume's explanation of the origin of the indirect passions depends on the idea that like impressions associate with each other and that like ideas associate with each other. A double relation, one between ideas and one between impressions, is necessary for the arousal of an indirect passion. Each indirect passion has a characteristic sensation and a characteristic object. The sensation of both pride and love is always pleasant and of humility and hatred always unpleasant. The characteristic object of love and hatred is always another person and of pride and humility always oneself. Thus for something to act as the cause of a particular indirect passion it has to be (a) capable of independently producing a feeling associated with the sensation characteristic of the passion, and (b) related to the characteristic object of the passion.

That cause, which excites the passion, is related to the object, which nature has attributed to the passion; the sensation, which the cause separately produces, is related to the sensation of the passion: From this double relation of ideas and impressions, the passion is deriv'd. (*Treatise*, p. 286.)

For example, reflection on something which I associate myself with (my house, my wife, my job) will arouse a feeling of pride if it produces pleasure but a feeling of shame or humility if it produces pain. If the object of my contemplation is associated with another person rather than myself then instead of pride or shame it will cause love or hatred.

I think it should be clear enough that Hume has inherited a Cartesian picture of emotional life. According to such a picture to experience an emotion is to recognize or perceive some inner mental event. Thus it is thought that an emotion is only causally connected with its object. The behaviour, verbal and non-verbal, and the bodily state of a person are seen as the symptoms or effects of this inner event to which he only has privileged and direct access. From the external effects the observer infers the existence of the emotion itself. Thus first-person psychological statements must be viewed as reports of introspective observations and third-person psychological statements as expressing inferences made as a result of some kind of inductive argument. Now for Hume the passions, like all impressions, are simple and unanalysable. Although he does make this distinction between the cause of a passion and its object, the connection between the object and its passion is only a contingent one. Anthony Kenny puts this very clearly:

It is because our minds happen to be made as they are that the object of pride is self, not because of anything involved in the concept of *pride*; just as it is because our bodies happen to be made as they are that our ears are lower than our eyes, not because of anything involved in the concept *ear*. A passion can be, and can be recognized as, pride before the idea of its object comes before the mind: the relation between the passion and this idea is one of cause and effect, and therefore, on Hume's general principles, a contingent one, inductively established. (*Action, Emotion and Will*, p. 24.)

That not only the connection between the passion and its object but also the connection between one passion and another is contingent is brought out in the following and, for Hume's whole approach to the subject, revealing passage:

According as we are possess'd with love or hatred, the correspondent desire of the happiness or misery of the person, who is the object of these passions, arises in the mind, and varies with each variation of these opposite passions. This order of things, abstractly consider'd, is not necessary. Love and hatred might have been unattended with any such desires, or their particular connexion might have been entirely revers'd. If nature had so pleas'd, love might have had the same effect as hatred, and hatred as love. I see no contradiction in supposing a desire of producing misery annex'd to love, and of happiness to hatred. (*Treatise*, p. 368.)

For Hume, to experience an emotion or passion consists in perceiving or recognizing some inner mental event. It is therefore *conceivable* that I might feel proud of something which I believed had absolutely no connection with myself or that I might love someone and yet hope for his unhappiness most of the time. The influence exerted by this Cartesianism is profound in Book Two; and in examining what Hume says there about sympathy we should bear it in mind all the time.

As I have said, Hume thinks of sympathy primarily as the principle which explains how feelings and opinions can be transferred from one individual to another. Typical of the passages in which this emerges are the following:

To this principle [of sympathy] we ought to ascribe the great uniformity we may observe in the humours and turn of thinking of those of the same nation; and 'tis much more probable, that this resemblance arises from sympathy, than from any influence of the soil and climate, which, tho' they continue invariably the same, are not able to preserve the character of a nation the same for a century together. A goodnatur'd man finds himself in an instant of the same humour with his company. . . . A chearful countenance infuses a sensible complacency and serenity into my mind; as an angry or sorrowful one throws a sudden damp upon me. Hatred, resentment, esteem, love, courage, mirth and melancholy; all these passions I feel more from communication than from my own natural temper and disposition. (*Treatise*, pp. 316–17.)

. . . the minds of men are mirrors to one another, not only because they reflect each others emotions, but also because those rays of passions, sentiments and opinions may be often reverberated, and may decay away by insensible degrees. (*Treatise*, p. 365.)

So close and intimate is the correspondence of human souls, that no sooner any person approaches me, than he diffuses on me all his opinions, and draws along my judgment in a greater or lesser degree. And tho', on many occasions, my sympathy with him goes not so far as entirely to change my sentiments, and way of thinking; yet it seldom is so weak as not to disturb the easy course of my thought, and give an authority to that opinion, which is recommended to me by his assent and approbation. (*Treatise*, p. 592.)

Sympathy is 'a very powerful principle in human nature' (*Treatise*, p. 618). It is the principle which explains our love and esteem for the rich and our contempt for the poor. In turn, the rich man and the poor man are correspondingly pleased or pained through sympathy with this esteem or contempt. It is in this sense that we are each 'mirrors' to one another. Sympathy also explains how beliefs, opinions, and attitudes are disseminated within a community. When we come to examine the account of the mechanism of sympathy we shall see that it is possible to interpret Hume's words fairly literally and to assimilate opinions and beliefs with passions. Moreover, the desire to be thought well of by others is conditional on some kind of sympathy. Finally, there is the role that sympathy plays in evaluation.

Now in the account of the mechanism of sympathy Hume is offering us an explanation of the causal mechanism governing the communication of passion and opinion from one person to another. This explanation relies ultimately on the theory of impressions and ideas. An impression, according to this theory, differs from its corresponding idea solely in terms of its liveliness. In short, sympathy consists of the conversion of an idea into its corresponding impression.

When any affection is infus'd by sympathy, it is at first known only by its effects, and by those external signs in the countenance and conversation, which convey an idea of it. This idea is presently converted into an impression, and acquires such a degree of force and vivacity, as to become the very passion itself, and produce an equal emotion, as any original affection. (*Treatise*, p. 317.)

Initially, my perception that another is, say, feeling anxious is an idea. But if I am to sympathize with this other person then this idea of anxiety must somehow be converted into an impression, or passion, of anxiety. Hume explains that this conversion is able to take place because of 'a quality in human nature' which is the capacity which an impression possesses for transfusing its native liveliness or vivacity into any ideas it should happen to be associated with. Thus my ideally-entertained passion, in so far as it is associated with some impression which acts as an enlivening source, will be converted into an impression, that is, an actual passion. This enlivening source is to be found, Hume maintains, in the agent's feeling of self-consciousness, his ever-present impression of self.

'Tis evident, that the idea, or rather impression of ourselves is always intimately present with us, and that our consciousness gives us so lively a conception of our own person, that 'tis not possible to imagine, that any thing can in this particular go beyond it. Whatever object, therefore, is related to ourselves must be conceived with a like vivacity of conception. (*Treatise*, p. 317.)

When we observe the outward signs or 'effects' of another's affection and so form an idea of this affection, the ease or difficulty with which this idea is converted into an impression will depend on the extent to which we associate ourselves with the other person: 'The stronger the relation is betwixt ourselves and any object, the more easily does the imagination make the transition, and convey to the related idea the vivacity of conception, with which we always form the idea of our own person.' (*Treatise*, p. 318.) The strength of the association between ourself and the other person is governed by the presence or absence of the relations of resemblance, contiguity, and cause and effect. But before discussing the role of these relations, I want to say something about the role which Hume assigns to self-consciousness or, as he terms it, the 'impression of ourselves . . . always intimately present with us' (*Treatise*, p. 317).

Hume has been taken to task several times on the ground that the role of the self in the doctrine of sympathy is inconsistent with what he teaches about self-identity in Book One. It is suggested that whereas in Book One Hume wants to deny that there can be an impression of the self, in his account of the genesis of sympathy he makes a direct appeal to what can only be this allegedly non-existent impression.[1] It is true that judging by the vagueness of many of the references to the self in the context of sympathy Hume himself is not too happy about his position; within the space of two pages (*Treatise*, pp. 317–18) the self is referred to as an 'idea', an 'impression', a 'conception', and

---

[1] See, for instance, F. Copleston, *A History of Philosophy*, vol. v, p. 128.

'consciousness'. Perhaps Kemp Smith (op. cit., p. 173) is correct in putting this indecisiveness down to the fact that Hume had worked out his moral theory, and with it the doctrine of sympathy, before the epistemological doctrines of Book One. Certainly, as he suggests in the same place, we are presumably justified in disregarding all but 'impression' in the context of sympathy; since it must be as an impression that the awareness of self must be continously with us; since in the mechanism of sympathy its function is to transfer its own native liveliness to the ideas associated with it; and it is only an impression *qua* impression which could perform such a function. Nevertheless, the criticism that the self in Book One is inconsistent with the self in Book Two is at least plausible when we take a passage such as this from Book One:

> For my part, when I enter most intimately into what I call *myself*, I always stumble upon some particular perception or other, of heat or cold, light or shade, love or hatred, pain or pleasure. I never can catch *myself* at any time without a perception, and never can observe anything but the perception. . . .
> But setting aside some metaphysicians of this kind, I may venture to affirm of the rest of mankind, that they are nothing but a bundle or collection of different perceptions, which succeed each other with an inconceivable rapidity, and are in a perpetual flux and movement. (*Treatise*, p. 252.)

and compare it with passages such as these from Book Two:

> Ourself is always intimately present to us. (*Treatise*, p. 320.)

> 'Tis evident, that the idea, or rather impression, of ourselves is always intimately present with us, and that our consciousness gives us so lively a conception of our own person, that 'tis not possible to imagine, that any thing can in this particular go beyond it. (*Treatise*, p. 317.)

But where Hume's critics go wrong is in failing to ask themselves what Hume's intention is in the Book One passage. In fact, Hume's aim there is to vindicate the common-sense belief in personal identity. His method of setting about this task is in conscious opposition to that of those contemporary philosophers who thought that through introspection they could demonstrate the existence of a simple, immutable self. Hume states the opposition's case as follows:

> There are some philosophers, who imagine that we are every moment intimately conscious of what we call our SELF; that we feel its

existence and its continuance in existence; and are certain, beyond the evidence of a demonstration, both of its perfect identity and simplicity. The strongest sensation, the most violent passion, say they, instead of distracting us from this view, only fix it the more intensely, and make us consider their influence on *self* either by their pain or pleasure. To attempt a farther proof of this were to weaken its evidence; since no proof can be deriv'd from any fact, of which we are so intimately conscious; nor is there any thing, of which we can be certain, if we doubt of this. (*Treatise*, p. 251.)

Hume thought that this kind of attempt to justify the belief in personal identity was utterly misguided and that the Cartesians were only deceiving themselves and others with them. So Hume threw out his challenge: If we are supposed to have an idea of some persisting and immutable self then what is its corresponding impression? If there were such an impression it would have to be constant and invariable. But no matter how diligently we intro-spect the only impressions we can discover, insisted Hume, are those of *particular mental states*. But if there is no impression of the self then it follows that there cannot be an idea of the self in the sense maintained. It is important to understand that the object of this argument of Hume's is to refute what he considered to be an unjustified claim. C. W. Hendel makes the following point:

That earlier description tells us only what we can *observe*, if we think that we can look upon mind directly, as an *object* of perception. But Hume disagrees with the 'metaphysicians' in their pretensions, and he states what they actually discover is *not* what they believe. (*Studies in the Philosophy of David Hume*, p. 213n.)

Hume suggests that very often we mistakenly ascribe a perfect identity to what is really a succession of closely related objects: we tend to 'feign some new and unintelligible principle, that con-nects the objects to-gether, and prevents their interruption and variation'. Thus we 'feign the continu'd existence of the percep-tions of the senses . . . and run into the notion of a *soul*, and *self*, and *substance*' (*Treatise*, p. 254). Hume accepts that there is a common-sense belief in the self and sees his task as that of show-ing, according to his principle of the association of ideas and impressions, how this belief comes about. If we want the true idea of the mind, Hume maintains, then we should

consider it as a system of different perceptions or different existences, which are link'd together by the relation of cause and effect, and mutually produce, destroy, influence, and modify each other. Our impressions give rise to their correspondent ideas; and these ideas in their turn produce other impressions. One thought chaces another, and draws after it a third, by which it is expell'd in its turn. In this respect, I cannot compare the soul more properly to any thing than to a republic or commonwealth, in which the several members are united by the reciprocal ties of government and subordination. . . . (*Treatise*, p. 261.)

We are not so much concerned with the merit of this analysis of mind as with its bearing on the role allotted to the self in the account of the genesis of sympathy. I think it should be clear enough by now that there is no inconsistency between Book One and Book Two on this score after all. Hume's scepticism is directed only at those who would claim to be able to discover the self as a unique, unchanging impression within themselves—not at the ordinary, everyday belief in personal identity we all share. Hume all along insists that the self is not an object of perception; and it is not as an object of perception that he considers the self to be part of the mechanism of sympathy.

We can now return to the part played by resemblance, contiguity, and the causal relation in the mechanism of sympathy. These relations function so as to strengthen the association between the agent's impression of self and the other person, thus enlivening the agent's idea of this other person's passion. Hume recognizes that sympathy comes more easily for us with those who in some way resemble ourselves; if there is 'any peculiar similarity in our manners, or characters, or country, or language, it facilitates the sympathy' (*Treatise*, p. 318). Moreover, the sentiments of others have little influence upon us when they are far away from us in time or place: it is a matter of common observation that we sympathize more with our neighbours than with those on the other side of the world, more with our contemporaries than those long dead. Such distances both in time and space can be counteracted, however, by the effect of such causal relations as blood propinquity and acquaintance. Now whilst all three relations function so as to strengthen the association of the agent's idea of the other's passion and the agent's impression of self, the causal relation seems to have a further function in the sympathetic mechanism. Hume says:

Resemblance and contiguity are relations not to be neglected; especially when by an inference from cause and effect, and by the observation of external signs, we are inform'd of the real existence of the object, which is resembling or contiguous. (*Treatise*, p. 317.)

For besides the relation of cause and effect, by which we are convinc'd of the reality of the passion, with which we sympathize; besides this, I say, we must be assisted by the relations of resemblance and contiguity, in order to feel the sympathy in its full perfection. (*Treatise*, p. 320.)

From these two passages it would appear that the relation of cause and effect functions so as to convince the agent of the 'reality' of the other person's passion. This is made clearer by the following passage from Book Three:

When I see the *effects* of passion in the voice and gesture of any person, my mind immediately passes from these effects to their causes, and forms such a lively idea of the passion, as is presently converted into the passion itself. In like manner, when I perceive the *causes* of any emotion, my mind is convey'd to the effects, and is actuated with a like emotion. Were I present at any of the more terrible operations of surgery, 'tis certain that even before it begun, the preparation of the instruments, the laying of the bandages in order, the heating of the irons, with all the signs of anxiety and concern in the patients and assistants, wou'd have a great effect upon my mind, and excite the strongest sentiments of pity and terror. No passion of another discovers itself immediately to the mind. We are only sensible of its causes or effects. From *these* we infer the passion: And consequently *these* give rise to our sympathy. (*Treatise*, p. 576.)

Here Hume is concerned not with how the idea of another's passion comes to be converted into the corresponding impression but with how the idea comes to be entertained in the first place. Hume recognizes that sympathy requires prior knowledge or belief about the other person's state of mind. But the minds of others are not accessible to direct inspection by anyone besides themselves. According to Hume's Cartesianism, to know what another is feeling entails either making an inference from an effect to its cause or from a cause to its effect. In the former case, I observe the effects of, say, fear in the demeanour and behaviour of another and from these I infer that he is frightened; and in the latter case, I observe the frightening circumstances of the other person and from these I infer that he is frightened. Since direct knowledge of another's state of mind is impossible, we have to rely for the knowledge we do have on a method of inductive inference. Without the relation of cause and effect we could never come to entertain the idea of another's state of mind and the subsequent conversion of this idea into the corresponding impression could never take place. It is for this reason, then, that Hume emphasizes the importance of the causal relation in the sympathetic mechanism. In general, we can say that whilst the relations of resemblance, contiguity, and (but to a lesser extent) cause and effect govern the conversion of the idea into the impression, the causal relation is a logical precondition of there being an idea of another person's state of mind at all.

Hume admits, though, that the mere fact that we realize that another person is suffering does not necessarily mean that we shall sympathize with him. For it may be the case that our natural self-centredness outweighs our realization of the other person's feelings so that instead of entering into his feelings we keep dwelling on ourselves with the result that we see the other's situation *only in comparison with our own*. On these occasions sympathy does not even get started. It is not just a question of not sympathizing fully: Hume insists that it is wrong to say that there is any sympathy at all.[1] The effect of comparison is 'directly contrary' to that of sympathy:

> We judge more of objects by comparison, than by their intrinsic worth and value; and regard everything as mean, when set in opposition to what is superior of the same kind. But no comparison is more obvious than that with ourselves; and hence it is that on all occasions it takes place, and mixes with most of our passions. This kind of comparison is directly contrary to sympathy in its operation. . . . *In all kinds of comparison an object makes us always receive from another, to which it is compar'd, a sensation contrary to what arises from itself in its direct and immediate survey. The direct survey of another's pleasure naturally gives us pleasure; and therefore produces pain, when compar'd with our own. His pain, consider'd in itself, is painful; but augments the idea of our own happiness, and gives us pleasure.* (*Treatise*, pp. 593–4.)

If I witness someone else enjoying himself then usually I am pleased at this; but if it should happen that I am already feeling miserable then the sight of another's happiness will, through comparison, only serve to plunge me deeper into my state of melancholy and self-pity. Similarly, although another's sufferings, when considered in themselves, will arouse my sympathy, when

---

[1] Cf. J. B. Stewart who interprets Hume as saying that sympathy *through comparison* may lead to envy and malice (*The Moral and Political Philosophy of David Hume*, p. 72).

considered in the light of my own circumstances, they may well
increase my own happiness. Hume invites me to suppose myself
on dry land whilst a storm is raging at sea. Now in order to make
myself appreciate my own good fortune I must turn my thoughts
to the desperate situation of those at sea. But no matter how hard
I try to imagine their situation, the comparison I thereby make
can never be as effective as it would be if I were really on the
shore watching a ship in great danger. But, more than this,
suppose

the ship to be driven so near me, that I can perceive distinctly the
horror, painted on the countenance of the seamen and passengers,
hear their lamentable cries, see the dearest friends give their last adieu,
or embrace with a resolution to perish in each others arms : No man
has so savage a heart as to reap any pleasure from such a spectacle, or
withstand the motions of the tenderest compassion and sympathy.
(*Treatise*, p. 594.)

For in such a case my idea of the suffering of these people has,
especially through the presence of the relation of contiguity, been
converted into the corresponding impression. Hume's general
conclusion is that if the idea of another's passion is too faint it
cannot even exert any influence on the agent's feelings by comparison; but that if it is very vivid it will affect him by sympathy
only. It is important to realize that it does not follow from what
Hume has said here that where there is sympathy there will always
be pity or compassion. As we shall presently see, on Hume's
account sympathy is still compatible with such passions as hatred
and contempt.[1]

To take stock of the account of sympathy so far. There seem
to be two distinct stages in the genesis of sympathy : (a) from my
observation of another's behaviour and manner I infer his state
of mind; and (b) the idea of the affection which I thus entertain
is converted into the corresponding impression. An example :
I see someone weeping and from this I infer that he is in some
kind of distress. In so far as I associate myself with him, my
ideally-entertained distress will be converted into an actual feeling
of distress. The extent to which I associate myself with him is
governed by the presence or absence of the three relations. If

---

[1] It is interesting to compare what Hume says about comparison with Bishop
Butler's suggestion that the sight of another's distress, even when it gives rise to
compassion or sympathy proper, always causes 'some degree of satisfaction from
a consciousness of our freedom from that misery' (*Fifteen Sermons*, p. 408n.).

this association is strong (suppose that the other person is a close friend or a member of the same family) than the vivacity possessed by the impression I always have of myself will be injected into my idea of distress with the result that it is raised to the corresponding impression, that is, an actual feeling of distress. When this occurs then it is correct to say that I 'sympathize' with the other person.

As it stands, several points may be made about this account.

(i) There is a discrepancy between my idea in stage (a) and my impression in stage (b). In stage (a) it is my idea of *another's* passion which I entertain, whilst in stage (b) it is my impression of that passion or, its equivalent, the passion itself which I experience. The whole mechanism relies on the theory that an idea differs from its corresponding impression only in degree. Clearly, then, it is only the idea of a passion as such (i.e. irrespective of who feels it) which is different in degree only from the impression of that passion or the passion itself. Strictly speaking, one can distinguish four elements in the sympathetic mechanism: (a) my idea of a particular passion; (b) my idea of this passion as belonging to another person; (c) my impression of self; and (d) my impression of the passion or the passion itself. It is (a) which is converted into (d) through the enlivening influence of (c); but the latter can only exert this influence in so far as it is associated with (b).

(ii) It is clear that on Hume's account we can only sympathize with feelings which we ourselves have already experienced.[1] If a passion is a simple impression and an idea a weak copy of an impression then it follows that my idea of a passion, even though someone else feels it, must be a copy of an impression which I have previously experienced myself.

(iii) In so far as Hume thinks that belief is merely a lively idea or impression, there can be no objections to saying that an idea that X is the case can, through being associated with an impression, be so enlivened as to become a belief that X is the case. It follows that beliefs, opinions, and attitudes are just as susceptible to communication from one person to another by means of the sympathetic mechanism as passions and emotions are. (For Hume's account of belief see Book One, Part III, for instance pp. 86, 98, 105–6.)

[1] For my discussion of the relation between past experience and sympathy see Chapter I, p. 9.

(iv) Perhaps, though, the most striking thing about Hume's account is its implication that when we sympathize with some-one's feelings we are supposed actually to experience those feel-ings; when I sympathize with someone's anxiety I have actually to feel anxious. True, Hume does say that initially my idea of the passion is 'conceiv'd to belong to another person, as we conceive any other matter of fact' (*Treatise*, p. 319); but he nowhere sug-gests that when we are sympathizing (as opposed to merely enter-taining the idea of the other's state of mind) we are at all conscious of the fact that our feelings are, as it were, 'not really our own'. On p. 317 Hume explicitly says that our idea is converted into 'the very passion itself'. Hume seems unable to make the distinc-tion between actually being, say, anxious and sympathizing with someone who is anxious. We should not normally think that sympathizing with someone who is anxious and depressed entails being anxious and depressed oneself. I might be depressed over or anxious about the other person's depression and anxiety (expecially if I knew him well or felt responsible for him) or I might be infected by his depression and anxiety; but both of these cases are quite distinct from the case where I sympathize with him in his depression and anxiety.

(v) That someone could come, by the mechanism of sympathy, to experience the same emotion or feeling as another is only plausible on the Cartesian suppositions that emotions and other feelings are private occurrences and that the relationship between an emotion or feeling and its object is a contingent one. If a financier is apprehensive about his gold shares what sense is there in supposing that another person can come to experience this same feeling? Yet Hume wants to deny that there is any difference between the financier's apprehension and the sympathetic agent's apprehension. This is only made acceptable if we can accept Hume's underlying Cartesianism. If, say, apprehension is a specific feeling which a subject can, by introspection, identify within himself and which is only contingently connected with the subject's circumstances, then it is presumably possible for me to experience this feeling of apprehension when I am in circum-stances which are not in the least apprehension-making. Only on such a theory does it make sense to suppose, as the sympathetic mechanism must suppose, that an agent could come literally to feel the same feeling as another without there being anything in his own circumstances to warrant this feeling.

As far as the genesis of sympathy goes, then, it appears that there is no question for Hume of sympathy involving an agent's imaginative realization of another's feelings. His notion of sympathy seems more akin to the instinctive response which is emotional infection than to the exercise involving imagination and self-consciousness which I suggested in the preceding chapter we should understand as the primary meaning of 'sympathy'. The equation between sympathy and infection or contagion runs as a distinct thread through the *Treatise*;[1] here are just a few instances :

A good-natur'd man finds himself in an instant of the same humour with his company. . . . (*Treatise*, p. 317.)

. . . observe the force of sympathy thro' the whole animal creation, and the easy communication of sentiments from one thinking being to another. (*Treatise*, p. 363.)

Every one has observ'd how much more dogs are animated in a pack than when they pursue their game apart; and 'tis evident that this can proceed from nothing but sympathy. (*Treatise*, p. 398.)

We may begin with considering a-new the nature and force of *sympathy*. The minds of men are similar in their feelings and operations, nor can any one be actuated by any affection, of which all others are not, in some degree, susceptible. As in strings equally wound up, the motion of one communicates itself to the rest; so all the affections pass readily from one person to another, and beget correspondent movements in every human creature. (*Treatise*, p. 575.)

From his account of the genesis of sympathy and the particular illustrations of sympathy he gives, it is clear that Hume thinks that 'sympathy' refers to an involuntary process over which we have no control. Since he sees sympathy primarily as a kind of infectious fellow-feeling it is only to be expected that he does not make provision in his account for any practical concern for the other person. Yet Hume is certainly aware that sympathy is connected in some way with such a concern. But he misconstrues the nature of this connection. In accordance with his method in Book Two, he sees the problem as how to show, according to the principle of the association of ideas and impressions, that sympathy with suffering can ever give rise to the passions of pity and benevolence. In other words, Hume sees the connection as a psychological instead of a logical one.

---

[1] This equation persists through Hume's writings as a whole, for instance: the essay *Of National Characters* (1742); *Enquiry Concerning the Principles of Morals* (1751), pp. 250–1; letter to Adam Smith, 28 July 1759 (*Letters*, vol. i, p. 313).

Now, according to Hume, the indirect passion of pity is a 'concern for . . . the misery of others, without any friendship . . . to occasion this concern' (*Treatise*, p. 369). Although in at least one place Hume talks about 'pity or a sympathy with pain' (*Treatise*, p. 385) he cannot mean that these are identical for he often recognizes that sympathy with pain need *not* necessarily lead to pity. Pity is a passion founded on sympathy with affliction and sorrow, but it must be thought of as distinct from this sympathy. The question which faces Hume is this: Why should sympathy with uneasiness give rise to pity rather than to hatred? Sympathy with another's suffering involves, on Hume's account, feeling uneasy oneself; why should this experience lead to a concern for the welfare of the sufferer rather than just to a desire to shun all contact with him? This question is particularly urgent in view of Hume's explanation of our love and esteem for the rich and powerful in terms of our sympathy with their satisfaction and our contempt for the poor and mean in terms of our sympathy with their misery (*Treatise*, pp. 357–62). Is it possible to reconcile this explanation with the very obvious fact that sympathy often does give rise to pity and benevolence? Hume tackles this problem in Book Two, Part II, section 9. To the question 'Why does sympathy in uneasiness ever produce any passion beside good-will and kindness?' he gives the following answer:

I have mention'd two different causes, from which a transition of passion may arise, viz. a double relation of ideas and impressions, and what is similar to it, a conformity in the tendency and direction of any two desires, which arise from different principles. Now I assert, that when a sympathy with uneasiness is weak, it produces hatred or contempt by the former cause; when strong, it produces love and tenderness by the latter. This is the solution of the foregoing difficulty, which seems so urgent. (*Treatise*, p. 385.)

On the face of the matter, this argument is far from convincing and seems to have been improvised especially to meet the 'foregoing difficulty'. There are several phrases in the passage which need clarifying, viz. (a) 'a transition of passion'; (b) 'a double relation of ideas and impressions'; (c) 'a conformity in the tendency and direction of any two desires, which arise from different principles'; and (d) 'strong' and 'weak' sympathy. I shall take each of these separately.

(a) In this context by 'transition of passion' Hume does not mean the transference or communication of a passion from one individual to another (i.e. sympathy), but rather the succession of passions belonging to one individual and the way in which one passion may give way to or give rise to another passion.

(b) 'The double relation of impressions and ideas' refers to the (now familiar) causal mechanism which governs the occurrence of all the indirect passions. For something to be the cause of an indirect passion it must be related to the object of the passion (either oneself or another person) and it must independently produce a feeling which is related by resemblance to the characteristic sensation of the passion. It is essential that both these relations (the first one of ideas and the second of impressions) should hold if something is to be the cause of an indirect passion. Now the satisfaction or uneasiness I feel may be caused either directly or sympathetically. Thus I may love or hate someone either because he is the direct cause of my pleasure or pain or because I sympathize with his own pleasure or pain. The latter case is the more complicated and involves my idea of another's passion being converted through sympathy into my impression of this passion. It follows from this account that if I sympathize with someone else's suffering the two conditions requisite for the occurrence of hatred are present.

(c) Hitherto, Hume has maintained that a passion possesses two properties: its object and its sensation (*Treatise*, p. 286). But now in the section under discussion Hume modifies this account. He draws attention to the fact that at least some passions are characteristically conative; that is, they are attended with appetites or desires or, as Hume calls them, 'impulses or directions'. To experience such a passion is not just to experience a particular feeling of pain or pleasure—it is also to be moved to act in a certain direction.

. . . 'tis not the present sensation alone or momentary pain or pleasure, which determines the character of any passion, but the whole bent or tendency of it from the beginning to the end. One impression may be related to another, not only when their sensations are resembling, as we have all along suppos'd in the preceding cases; but also when their impulses or directions are similar and correspondent. (*Treatise*, p. 381.)

Passions may be related to one another not only through their characteristic sensations but also through their characteristic conations. Of the four important indirect passions, pride and humility, being 'pure sensations', are not conative in this sense;

by contrast, love and hatred are attended by, respectively, benevolence and anger. It is for this reason that pity is related to benevolence and anger to malice. Although pity involves the agent feeling uneasy himself, it is also 'a desire of happiness to another, and aversion to his misery' (*Treatise*, p. 382). In so far as benevolence is also a desire for the happiness of another and an aversion to his misery, Hume concludes that pity must be related to benevolence. So although, at first sight, pity, being an uneasy sensation, should be related to hatred, once we take into account the conative aspect of pity it becomes possible to explain why pity is not usually associated with hatred. Hume offers us a similar argument to show why malice, despite being a pleasure, is connected with anger and does not produce love. If we can for the moment accept Hume's arguments then he has shown why we do not hate those whom we pity—but he has still to show why we pity and feel benevolent towards those with whose suffering we sympathize. This is the really vital question; and here Hume's argument turns on his distinction between 'strong' and 'weak' sympathy or, as he later terms it, between 'extensive' and 'limited' sympathy.

(d) The difference between 'limited' and 'extensive' sympathy is that in 'limited' sympathy the agent is only aware of what the other person is feeling at that particular time whilst in 'extensive' sympathy the agent is aware both of this and what *might* happen to the other person. But this awareness of the other's possible future circumstances is not identical with benevolence or a concern for his welfare. Whether or not sympathy is extensive in this sense depends upon the vivacity with which the agent initially conceives the idea of the other's passion. The more vivid this initial idea, the greater the number of related ideas, among them the contingent circumstances of the other person, conceived.

When the present misery of another has any strong influence upon me, the vivacity of the conception is not confin'd merely to its immediate object, but diffuses its influence over all the related ideas, and gives me a lively notion of all the circumstances of that person, whether past, present, or future; possible, probable, or certain. By means of this lively notion I am interested in them; take part with them; and feel a sympathetic motion in my breast, conformable to whatever I imagine in his. If I diminish the vivacity of the first conception, I diminish that of the related ideas; as pipes can convey no more water than what arises at the fountain. (*Treatise*, p. 386.)

But if my initial conception of the other's passion is feeble then correspondingly my sympathy will be limited to the present and immediate:

> I may feel the present impression, but carry my sympathy no farther, and never transfuse the force of the first conception into my ideas of the related objects. If it be another's misery, which is presented in this feeble manner, I receive it by communication, and am affected by all the passions related to it: But as I am not so much interested as to concern myself in his good fortune, as well as his bad, I never feel the extensive sympathy, nor the passions related to *it*. (*Treatise*, p. 386.)

Now, according to Hume, the passion which is characteristically related to extensive sympathy is benevolence. In this context he refers to benevolence as 'an original pleasure arising from the pleasure of the person belov'd, and a pain proceeding from his pain' and 'a subsequent desire of his pleasure and aversion to his pain' (*Treatise*, p. 387). The crux of Hume's argument seems to consist of the suggestion that if sympathy is to give rise to benevolence it must be sympathy with *both* the other's pain *and* his pleasure:

> In order, then, to make a passion [*sic*] run parallel with benevolence, 'tis requisite we shou'd feel these double impressions, correspondent to those of the person, whom we consider; nor is any one of them alone sufficient for that purpose. (*Treatise*, p. 387.)

When sympathy is extensive it is not just the present pain or pleasure of the other person with which we sympathize but also his future pain or pleasure. It is in this double correspondence of impressions that my extensive sympathy is related to benevolence and hence to pity. By contrast, a weak sympathetic impression does not make us sensitive to the future condition of the other person; and if this impression is an unpleasant one it is related, by virtue of the resemblance of sensations, only to anger and hatred. 'Benevolence, therefore, arises from a great degree of misery, or any degree strongly sympathiz'd with: Hatred or contempt from a small degree, or one weakly sympathiz'd with.' (*Treatise*, p. 387.)

It is not at all clear, though, exactly how Hume wants to relate extensive sympathy to benevolence. The argument in this particular section of the *Treatise* is very confused but I shall try to make some sense out of it. Although Hume writes as if they are identical, I think that we must distinguish between the 'impulse' or 'direction' of a passion and its 'bent or tendency from the beginning to the end'. As I have previously suggested, the 'impulse' or 'direction' of a passion refers to its conative element. On the other hand, what the 'bent or tendency' of a passion refers to, if it is not the same thing, is unclear. The example we are given is 'the double correspondence of impressions' (not to be confused with 'the double relation of ideas and impressions'). But it is in respect of this property or characteristic ('the double correspondence of impressions') that extensive sympathy and benevolence resemble one another. Hume's argument amounts to the following. In extensive sympathy if the other person suffers (even in my imagination) then I suffer and if he is happy (even in my imagination) then I am happy. Therefore such sympathy involves what may be called 'a double correspondence of impressions'. Benevolence is a passion which can be analysed into 'an original pleasure arising from the pleasure of the person belov'd, and a pain proceeding from his pain' (i.e. its 'bent or tendency') together with 'a desire of his pleasure and an aversion to his pain' (i.e. its 'impulse' or conation). Thus the 'bent or tendency' of benevolence can be described as 'a double correspondence of impressions'. Therefore in so far as both extensive sympathy and benevolence exhibit this 'double correspondence of impressions', the 'bent or tendency' of the one will resemble that of the other. This means that if sympathy with uneasiness is sufficiently extensive it will, through the likeness of its 'bent or tendency' to that of benevolence, arouse in the agent this passion (and with it pity) rather than hatred and loathing.

But all that Hume has done is to perform a little sleight-of-hand. He wants to show a connection between sympathy and certain conations. So he posits this passion of 'benevolence' which conveniently turns out to possess just the required conations and which is related to a special kind of sympathy by virtue of this mysterious property, its 'bent or tendency'. But what is the difference between benevolence and extensive sympathy if it is not the former's possession of these conative elements? It is still open to ask why benevolence should be attended by a desire for the other's good and an aversion to his harm. I think this criticism is strengthened by the fact that Hume equivocates as to what he does mean by 'benevolence'; on p. 382 it is the 'appetite' which attends love; but on p. 387 it has become an 'original' pleasure and pain arising out of the beloved person's pleasure and pain.

As I have said, Hume's discussion is not very clear; but I cannot see a stronger interpretation than this one. If, for instance, no distinction were made between the 'impulse' and the 'bent or tendency' of a passion then his argument would only beg the question even more blatantly.

Hume's efforts to relate sympathy to the passions of benevolence and pity, if anything, only serve to emphasize the inadequacy of his initial concept of sympathy. It is too much to expect that Hume should have realized that 'sympathy' entailed having a benevolent disposition towards the other person, since this would have been alien to his whole method of inquiry in Book Two. We may wonder, though, if passions such as love and hatred are attended by characteristic appetites, why this should not be the case with sympathy; why benevolence should not be attached to sympathy 'by a natural and original quality'. There are at least two answers to this. One is that Hume did not see sympathy as a passion or emotion. Being the communication of passion, sympathy itself cannot possess the properties of a passion, such as appetite and sensation. (In so far as Hume appeals, in his explanation of the connection between extensive sympathy and benevolence, to the 'bent or tendency' of extensive sympathy, he is inconsistent—for this is surely to treat sympathy as a passion after all.) A second reason is that Hume's fundamental picture of sympathy as infectious fellow-feeling means that sympathy is compatible both with an attitude of concern and with one of indifference or even loathing and contempt. Had Hume suggested that benevolence was attached to sympathy 'by a natural and original quality' then he would have to revise this fundamental view and with it his whole psychology of the passions.[1]

However, to leave the impression that Hume's concept of sympathy is exclusively limited to infection is not completely accurate. For in the notion of 'extensive' sympathy he does seem to be putting forward a broader conception of sympathy than I have suggested up to now. The reason why I have avoided emphasizing this is because to have done so would have undermined from the very start this particular discussion of Hume's about the connection between sympathy and practical attitudes.

[1] In fact, in the *Enquiry Concerning the Principles of Morals* Hume does away with the whole mechanism of sympathy and with it the need to show a connection between sympathy and benevolence. In its place he puts the 'sentiment of humanity' or benevolence—an original and natural passion by which we are concerned for those with whom we have fellow-feeling. (See Appendix II, pp. 295–302.)

In so far as 'extensive' sympathy is merely thought of as a double correspondence of impressions then it is in fact just as compatible with hatred or indifference as infection is. But Hume says more than this. In 'extensive' sympathy the agent is not only sensitive to all the circumstances which are possible for the other person but he is also stated to be 'concerned' in the other's good fortune and 'interested' in all his circumstances (*Treatise*, p. 386). Thus it is possible to interpret Hume here as meaning that to 'sympathize' with a person necessarily involves being practically concerned for him. However, in the context of the *Treatise* any such suggestion that sympathy and practice are logically connected is ultimately undermined by Hume's fundamental misconception (as shown in the account of the genesis of sympathy) of the nature of the fellow-feeling which would be entailed by this practical sympathy. Hume does not realize that for fellow-feeling to form the ground of practical sympathy the agent who experiences this fellow-feeling must be aware of the subjectivity of the other person. But if fellow-feeling is merely the result of being infected by another's feelings then this awareness is not required. In Hume's genesis of sympathy, although when we initially conceive the idea of another's state of mind we have to be aware of his separate autonomous existence, once this idea has been converted by the psychological mechanism into the corresponding impression there is no necessity on the part of the agent for any regard for this other, any acknowledgement of his existence. Furthermore, Hume is not consistent about the meaning he puts upon 'extensive' sympathy. The following passage from Book Three seems specifically to deny that 'extensive' sympathy entails concern for the other person:

Upon these principles we may easily remove any contradiction, which may appear to be betwixt the *extensive sympathy*, on which our sentiments of virtue depend, and that *limited generosity* which I have frequently observ'd to be natural to men, and which justice and property suppose. . . . My sympathy with another may give me the sentiment of pain and disapprobation, when any object is presented, that has a tendency to give him uneasiness; tho' I may not be willing to sacrifice any thing of my own interest, or cross any of my passions, for his satisfaction. (*Treatise*, p. 586.)

I may sympathize with another's uneasiness but this does not mean that I should go out of my way to remove the cause of his uneasiness.

Finally, a few words about sympathy and egoism. It seems to me that Hume's doctrine of sympathy is unduly egocentric in three respects. (a) To sympathize with another means, according to Hume, that the agent must experience the actual feeling which the other person is feeling. (b) We can only sympathize with those feelings which we have previously experienced on our own account. (c) We need have no regard for the other person once the mechanism of sympathy has worked. But to say that the doctrine of sympathy is unduly egocentric in these respects is not to say that the doctrine of sympathy goes any way to showing that Hume's philosophy of mind as a whole is unduly egoistic. The criticism that Hume is a psychological hedonist has a pedigree stretching back at least as far as T. H. Green's *Introduction*.[1] In its most common form it would allege that Hume's doctrines imply that all conduct is ultimately motivated by the agent's desire for his own pleasure and that there is no such thing as disinterested benevolence. But the doctrine of sympathy does nothing to support this criticism; it does not suggest that we cannot be concerned for the happiness of another except as a means to our own happiness. But I do not intend to embark on a discussion of this criticism of Hume; I have only mentioned it in order that it will not be confused with the altogether distinct claim that the doctrine of sympathy is unduly egocentric.

On the combined evidence of (a) Hume's account of the genesis of sympathy, (b) his failure to reconcile sympathy and benevolence, and (c) his illustrations of the working of sympathy, I think we are justified in concluding that his concept of sympathy is a limited, virtually technical, one. Apart from the relatively few passages where he talks about 'extensive' sympathy, we can say that Hume uses 'sympathy' to refer exclusively to a special kind of transference of emotion and other feeling from one person to another. No concern for the other person is implied by this sense. Of the various concepts of fellow-feeling discussed in the opening chapter, it appears to be identical with that of infectious fellow-feeling. In the following chapter I wish to examine how this concept of sympathy functions in the moral philosophy of the third book of the *Treatise*.

[1] For a recent statement of this criticism see D. G. C. MacNabb (op. cit., pp. 187-8).

III

SYMPATHY IN HUME'S MORAL PHILOSOPHY

THE concept of sympathy is ethically interesting in at least two different ways. In the more obvious of these ways sympathy is thought of as a *motive* for action. But Hume is not interested in this possibility. For him the significance of sympathy lies in its possibility of functioning as, what I am calling, the *medium* of moral judgement. It is therefore natural for Hume to concentrate his attention not on the agent's sympathetic motive but on the spectator's sympathetic response. This preoccupation with the spectator of the moral situation is in accordance with the passive and non-practical aspect of Hume's concept of sympathy.

To begin, it is essential to be clear about the exact nature of Hume's inquiry in Book Three of the *Treatise*. According to the theory presented in this book, moral distinctions are made in accordance with certain special, unanalysable feelings. Hume sees his task as that of giving a causal account of the origin of these feelings. This comes out in the following key passage :

> . . . in all enquiries concerning these moral distinctions, it will be sufficient to shew the principles, which make us feel a satisfaction or uneasiness from the survey of any character, in order to satisfy us why the character is laudable or blameable. An action, or sentiment, or character is virtuous or vicious; why? because its view gives a pleasure or uneasiness of a particular kind. In giving a reason, therefore, for the pleasure or uneasiness, we sufficiently explain the vice or virtue. (*Treatise*, p. 471.)

From this it appears that Hume believes that the moral feelings are susceptible to the same kind of psychological explanation as that which in Book Two he offers for the indirect passions. In his study, *Passion and Value in Hume's Treatise*, Páll S. Árdal maintains that many commentators on the *Treatise* have unduly emphasized the inconsistencies between Books Two and Three and have failed to recognize the essential unity of thought which lies behind these two books. In particular they have failed to see the close connection between the doctrine of the indirect passions in Book Two and the account of moral approval and disapproval in Book Three. Árdal suggests that the moral feelings should be considered as objective variants of the indirect passions (op. cit., pp. 109–47). This interpretation seems to me to be especially helpful for coming to understand how sympathy fits into Hume's moral theory.

It is well known that the major thesis of Book Three is that moral evaluation depends in some sense upon feeling or sentiment. Those mental qualities or characteristics in others which when contemplated by a spectator arouse in him feelings of uneasiness, pain, or disgust are called 'vicious' whilst those which so arouse feelings of pleasure or satisfaction are called 'virtuous' (*Treatise*, p. 591). Obviously, this pleasure and pain cannot be any kind of pleasure and pain; for not everything which pleases is morally good just as not everything which pains is necessarily morally bad. What counts, says Hume, is pleasure and pain of a 'particular kind' (*Treatise*, p. 471). He suggests that we distinguish the pleasure and pain which is morally relevant from that which is not in two distinct ways. In the first place, moral and non-moral pleasure and pain feel *qualitatively* different:

. . . 'tis evident that under the term *pleasure*, we comprehend sensations, which are very different from each other, and which have only such a distant resemblance, as is requisite to make them be express'd by the same abstract term. A good composition of music and a bottle of good wine equally produce pleasure; and what is more, their goodness is determin'd merely by the pleasure. But shall we say upon that account, that the wine is harmonious, or the music of a good flavour? In like manner, an inanimate object, and the character or sentiments of any person may, both of them, give satisfaction; but as the satisfaction is different, this keeps our sentiments concerning them from being confounded, and makes us ascribe virtue to the one, and not to the other. (*Treatise*, p. 472.)

The pleasure that the contemplation of a good man arouses in us feels intrinsically different from the pleasure that is derived from listening to a good piece of music or drinking a good bottle of wine. Although on the one hand the two kinds of feeling sufficiently resemble each other to justify the use of the one word 'pleasure' in both cases, on the other hand experience teaches us that there is a clear distinction between the kind of feeling which the contemplation of human agents—their actions, emotions, and dispositions—arouses in us and the kind of feeling which the contemplation of inanimate objects arouses in us. This is why, Hume thinks, there is no question of our ever becoming confused and thinking of inanimate objects as virtuous or vicious. The second basis for the distinction between moral and non-moral pain and pleasure is to be found, Hume suggests, in the attitude of the spectator himself, that is, the person who is making the judgement. The passage quoted above continues:

> Nor is every sentiment of pleasure or pain, which arises from characters and actions, of that *peculiar* kind, which makes us praise or condemn. The good qualities of an enemy are hurtful to us; but may still command our respect and esteem. 'Tis only when a character is consider'd in general, without reference to our particular interest, that it causes such a feeling or sentiment, as denominates it morally good or evil. (Ibid.)

Although the moral feelings can only arise on the contemplation of another person's character and conduct, the feelings which are aroused on such occasions are not bound to be moral feelings. If a man is my enemy or rival then a contemplation of, say, his ambition, courage or efficiency is hardly likely to give me much satisfaction. But from an impersonal point of view it always remains open for me to admire in him those very qualities which in competition with him may cause my own defeat. The possibility of this kind of admiration or approval depends on my having ignored my own interests for the moment or, in other words, on my having adopted an impartial and general point of view. It is Hume's contention that *only if we adopt such an objective standpoint* can our subsequent feelings amount to moral approval or disapproval: if we fail to adopt this attitude then our feelings will be merely those of liking or disliking, loving or hating. This idea of adopting a general point of view will be discussed more fully later on; for the present what we should note is that the feelings which constitute moral approval and disapproval are not immediate responses to a situation but are, on the contrary, the outcome of reflection on that situation.

Although love and hate differ from approval and disapproval in so far as the former are biased and the latter objective, the moral feelings do exhibit certain important characteristics in common with the indirect passions. Like the indirect passions (and for that matter all passions), the moral feelings are (a) simple and unanalysable, and (b) subject to the laws of association. Given these assumptions, it is reasonable to suppose that the moral feelings must be susceptible to the same kind of causal explanation of their origins as that offered for the indirect passions.

We recall that an indirect passion can only be aroused when there is a double relation of ideas and impressions. Thus for a quality or characteristic to act as the cause of an indirect passion it has (a) independently to produce a sensation which resembles the sensation characteristic of the indirect passion (this will be the relation of impressions), and (b) to be associated with the object of the indirect passion, that is, either oneself or another (this will constitute the relation of ideas). For example, when I contemplate a rich man I sympathize with the pleasure he derives (or I suppose he derives) from his possessions. This sympathetic pleasure is associated by resemblance with the pleasant sensation characteristic of love. At the same time, my attention being directed towards another person, the further relation of ideas will hold between this other person and the object of love (which is always another). In so far as my contemplation of the rich man will bring about these two separate associations for me, it will cause me to love the rich man.

It follows directly from this account that the indirect passions must be capable of being aroused by the moral feelings. Hume seems to make this point in the following passage towards the end of the first part of Book Three:

Pride and humility, love and hatred are excited, when there is any thing presented to us, that both bears a relation to the object of the passion, and produces a separate sensation related to the sensation of the passion. Now virtue and vice are attended with these circumstances. They must necessarily be plac'd in ourselves or others, and excite either pleasure or uneasiness; and therefore must give rise to one of these four passions. (*Treatise*, p. 473.)

Approval and disapproval fulfil the conditions necessary if something is to act as the cause of an indirect passion; that is, they are attended by the appropriate 'circumstances'. When I describe someone as 'virtuous' then, according to Hume, I do this in accordance with a particular feeling of pleasure which the contemplation of this other person has produced in me. This pleasant sensation must be related by resemblance to the pleasant sensation characteristic of both love and pride. In so far as my attention is focused exclusively on the other person I shall love him; but in so far as I associate myself with him (if, for instance, I think of him as my pupil or my brother) this feeling of love will give way to or mingle with one of pride. A similar account of the relation between disapproval and hatred and humility can be given. Thus we shall tend to love the man we judge virtuous and hate the man we judge vicious; and we shall tend to feel proud when we ourselves or those with whom we associate ourselves act well and ashamed when we ourselves or our associates act badly.

It is easy to pick holes in Hume's position here. For instance, although a fairly plausible case can be made out for a connection between, on the one hand, pride and humility (in so far as the latter is equivalent to shame and remorse) and, on the other, moral disapproval, it is clear that we do not necessarily love where we approve or hate where we disapprove. The awkwardness of Hume's position is due not to faulty observation but to the rigidity of his psychology of association. But I do not want to dwell on this. What is of greater importance for the proper grasp of Hume's moral theory is to notice an ambiguity in the passage just quoted. When Hume says that 'vice and virtue are attended' with the same 'circumstances' as the indirect passions, he may be thought of as saying either (a) that the moral feelings themselves must always act as causes of the indirect passions (i.e. the interpretation I have already suggested), or (b) that anything which acts as a cause of a moral feeling must necessarily act as a cause of one or other of the indirect passions. In other words, by 'virtue and vice' Hume could mean the feelings of approval and disapproval themselves or the objects of these feelings. If we read the passage in terms of interpretation (b) then we shall see Hume as suggesting there is an analogy between the causes of the moral feelings and the causes of the indirect passions. Which interpretation is the correct one is really immaterial. Each is compatible with the other. The first must follow from Hume's analysis of the moral feelings taken together with his account of the genesis of the indirect passions; and as for the second, I shall shortly show that there is further evidence to suggest that the moral feelings are basically of the same mode of origin as the indirect passions. Welding (a) and (b) together, we could suggest Hume as saying that if someone already the object of an indirect passion becomes the subject of a moral judgement then the moral feeling in accordance with which this judgement is made will function as an additional cause of the indirect passion so as to prolong or intensify it. For example, if for some reason I come to approve of someone I already love then this feeling of approval will reinforce my love for this person.

This further evidence for the analogy between the moral feelings and the indirect passions is to be found at the beginning of the third part of Book Three, in a passage where Hume is insisting that the proper objects of praise and blame can only be settled dispositions or 'motives'. It is worth quoting the particular passage at length in order to show to what extent the indirect passions (especially love and hatred) and the moral feelings are bracketed together in Hume's thought:

> If any *action* be either virtuous or vicious, 'tis only as a sign of some quality or character. It must depend upon durable principles of the mind, which extend over the whole conduct, and enter into the personal character. *Actions themselves, not proceeding from any constant principles have no influence on love or hatred, pride or humility; and consequently are never consider'd in morality.*[1]
>
> This reflexion is self-evident, and deserves to be attended to, as being of the utmost importance in the present subject. We are never to consider any single action in our enquiries concerning the origin of morals; but only the quality or character from which the action proceeded. These alone are *durable* enough to affect our sentiments concerning the person. Actions are, indeed, better indications of a character than words, or even wishes and sentiments; but 'tis only so far as they are such indications, that they are attended with love or hatred, praise or blame.
>
> To discover the true origin of morals, and of that love or hatred, which arises from mental qualities, we must take the matter pretty deep. . . . (*Treatise*, p. 575.)

By 'durable principles of the mind' Hume must mean character-traits like generosity, impatience, frankness, and thoughtfulness. Although we commonly talk about *actions* as being virtuous or vicious, strictly speaking this is incorrect; for actions are only the external 'signs' of the agent's character. The proper object of praise and blame is therefore the 'motive' which 'produced' the action (cf. *Treatise*, p. 477). In Hume's terminology to give a 'motive' for an action is to assign an exciting cause to it. According to Hume's theory of causation, for X to be the cause of Y we must have experienced the constant conjunction of X and Y. It is therefore not surprising to find this emphasis placed on the view that we form our opinions of others on the basis of what we

---

[1] My italics.

take to be their permanent characters. The corollary of this view
is that to say that someone acted 'out of character' is to reduce his
responsibility for his behaviour, to offer an excuse for him
(*Treatise*, p. 411). But now to come on to the main reason for
quoting this extract. The key sentence is:

Actions themselves, not proceeding from any constant principle,
have no influence on love or hatred, pride or humility; and consequently are never consider'd in morality.

That is, Hume is here arguing that because actions cannot cause
indirect passions they cannot cause moral feelings. The assumption behind this argument must be that the causes of the moral
feelings are similar to the causes of the indirect passions. The
analogy is further substantiated by reference to a passage almost
at the end of the *Treatise* where Hume says that 'approbation or
blame . . . is nothing but a fainter and more imperceptible love
or hatred' (*Treatise*, p. 614). That is, he is contrasting the calmness
of the moral feelings with the violence of the indirect passions of
love and hatred. (The qualities of calmness and violence refer to
the intensity with which the passion is felt.) The implication of this
statement is, once again, that the moral feelings originate in the
same way as the indirect passions do.

If we can accept the existence of this analogy between the
moral feelings and the indirect passions then it is clear why sympathy is so important in Hume's account of what it is to make
a moral judgement. In the explanation of why we love the rich
man and hate the poor man sympathy plays a vital role; and in the
explanation of how the contemplation of the behaviour and
character of others causes feelings of approval and disapproval
in the spectator there is an analogous reliance on sympathy.
Approval and disapproval are feelings of, respectively, pleasure
and pain. It is obvious that our immediate, selfish feelings are not
morally relevant. The only way in which we can come to be concerned with what is conducive to the happiness of others but
not ourselves is, Hume believes, through sympathy. Through
this principle what gives others pleasure and pain also gives us—
the spectators—pleasure and pain.

. . . moral distinctions arise, in a great measure, from the tendency
of qualities and characters to the interests of society, and . . . 'tis our
concern for that interest, which makes us approve or disapprove of
them. Now we have no such extensive concern for society but from

sympathy; and consequently 'tis that principle, which takes us so far out of ourselves, as to give us the same pleasure or uneasiness in the characters of others, as if they had a tendency to our own advantage or loss. (*Treatise*, p. 579.)

It is important to distinguish between the spectator's moral feeling and his sympathy. The moral feeling is *not* in any sense a species of sympathy or sympathetic feeling.[1] The object of the sympathy is quite distinct from the object of the approval or disapproval.[2] This should be clear enough if we bear in mind the model of the indirect passions. The spectator sympathizes with the feelings of either the agent or those who are affected by the agent's conduct; but the object of the spectator's approval or disapproval is the agent himself (his character and behaviour). As with the indirect passions, the double association of ideas and impressions must be present. The relation of impressions consists in the association through resemblance between the spectator's sympathetic pleasure or pain and, as the case may be, the pleasant sensation of approval or the unpleasant sensation of disapproval. The relation of ideas consists in the association between the idea of another or oneself and the object of the moral feelings which is always either another or oneself. If approval and disapproval of *others* are seen as objective variants of love and hatred, it is reasonable to see approval and disapproval of *oneself* as objective variants of pride and humility.

Up to a point, then, the explanation which Hume gives of the origins of the four indirect passions may be considered to be the model for the explanation of the origins of the moral feelings. Where the explanations diverge is at the point where the element of objectivity which is necessary for moral judgement is introduced.

Consider, for instance, Hume's account of the (artificial) virtue of justice. According to this account (*Treatise*, pp. 498–500), the original motive for the establishment of the notion of justice is interest. Men observe that their natural selfishness and limited generosity incapacitate them for society. To combat this the notion of justice is developed. Its basis is not a promise or contract (for these would presuppose justice) but rather a mutual agreement: men co-operate in its formation in much the same way as two men pull on the oars of a boat together—that is, by tacit

---

[1] Cf. T. H. Green who wrote that the moral sentiment must be 'a kind of sympathy' (*Works*, vol. i, pp. 357–8).

[2] For a discussion of this distinction see B. Wand's 'A Note on Sympathy in Hume's Moral Theory', *Philosophical Review* (1955).

consent. But whilst the original motive for its formation is interest, it is only by reference to sympathy that we account for the fact that the idea of *virtue* is attached to the observance of the rules of justice. Acts which we judge to be contrary to the rules of justice displease us because we consider them to be prejudicial to the good of society; but it is only through sympathy that we are interested in this good. Even though we ourselves are un-affected by particular acts of justice or injustice, we still sympa-thize with the satisfaction or uneasiness of those who are directly involved. And since those things the contemplation of which arouses in the spectator feelings of pleasure or satisfaction are denominated 'virtuous', justice is considered a virtue and the observance of its rules attended with the idea of obligation. As Hume puts it:

... when the injustice is so distant from us, as no way to affect our interest, it still displeases us; because we consider it as prejudicial to human society, and pernicious to everyone that approaches the person guilty of it. We partake of their uneasiness by *sympathy*; and as every thing, which gives uneasiness in human actions, upon the general sur-vey, is call'd Vice, and whatever produces satisfaction, in the same manner, is denominated Virtue; this is the reason why the sense of moral good and evil follows upon justice. . . . (*Treatise*, p. 499.)

But now to come on to the question of the objectivity of moral judgement, notice how careful Hume is to qualify the last sentence of the above extract by the phrase 'upon the general survey'. Although sympathy enlarges the scope of our emotional life, it does not free us of our self-centredness or built-in bias for our-selves. If we have a previous interest in the other person our sympathy with him will be prejudiced. Sympathy (and we must remember all the while that we are using the word in this context in Hume's sense) is capricious and lacks principle. Both the scope and intensity of my sympathy are affected by the relation which the other person bears to me; for instance, whether he is a friend or an enemy, an acquaintance or a stranger, whether I read about him in a history book or a newspaper, whether his conduct injures me or benefits me, and so on. Hume emphasizes this point in Book Two. But there is a general belief that moral evaluation should display consistency and be untouched by such factors. How then can we reconcile the capriciousness of sympathy with the ethical requirement of consistency? The variation of sympathy with the stability of esteem?

To meet this difficulty Hume explains that the spectator's sympathy can only give rise to moral feelings if he has first adopted
a point of view which is general and excludes all reference to
himself and his own interests:

> In order, therefore, to prevent those continual *contradictions* and
> arrive at a more *stable* judgement of things, we fix on some *steady* and
> *general* points of view; and always, in our thoughts, place ourselves in
> them, whatever may be our present situation. (*Treatise*, p. 581.)

Hume draws an analogy with the senses. A beautiful face does
not give us so much pleasure at twenty yards as at two; but we
do not for that reason say that the face is not beautiful whenever
we do not happen to be close to it. Experience teaches us to make
the appropriate adjustment. Similarly, we can learn to 'correct'
our immediate tendencies to blame and praise others, distorted
as these are by our particular situation. Without this habit of
judging others (and ourselves) objectively, we should be so much
at odds with each other that it would be impossible even to hold
an ordinary conversation. Our motive for acquiring the habit is
as much as anything a desire for convenience. If on an occasion
we should find it too difficult a task to ignore our personal
involvement, then, so long as we realize this, we can make due
allowance for it in what we say and think, using as a guide knowledge of the sorts of things we have approved and disapproved of
in the past.

> . . . these variations we regard not in our general decisions, but still
> apply the terms expressive of our liking or dislike, in the same manner,
> as if we remain'd in one point of view. Experience soon teaches us this
> method of correcting our sentiments, or at least, of correcting our
> language, where the sentiments are more stubborn and inalterable.
> (*Treatise*, p. 582.)

To take upon ourselves this role of the disinterested spectator
means that we must be concerned exclusively with the satisfaction
or uneasiness of the moral agent himself together with that of
those most immediately affected by his conduct. We can make
allowance for 'a certain degree of selfishness in men' (*Treatise*,
p. 583); and we can even go so far as not to blame a man 'for
opposing us in any of our pretensions'.

> . . . in judging of characters, the only interest or pleasure, which
> appears the same to every spectator, is that of the person himself,
> whose character is examin'd; or that of persons, who have a connexion

with him. And tho' such interests and pleasures touch us more faintly than our own, yet being more constant and universal, they counter-ballance the latter even in practice, and are alone admitted in specula-tion as the standard of virtue and morality. *They alone produce that particular feeling or sentiment, on which moral distinctions depend.*[1] (*Treatise*, p. 591.)

Hume thus replies to the objection that sympathy varies without a corresponding variation in moral esteem by distinguishing between (a) *immediate* sympathy and (b) sympathy *from a dis-interested standpoint*. The moral feelings are caused exclusively by disinterested sympathy. Since my immediate sympathetic feelings do not necessarily run parallel with my moral feelings, there is no contradiction in supposing that I may say, on the one hand, that I strongly sympathize with someone and yet, on the other hand, express disapproval of him.[2]

A second objection which Hume deals with is that we approve and disapprove of personal qualities even though the circum-stances in which the subject of these qualities happens to find himself prevent these qualities from actually being displayed or put to any purpose. 'Virtue in rags is still virtue.' (*Treatise*, p. 584.) But one would think that if a quality were stillborn in this way, the objection runs, so that no-one could derive any pleasure or benefit from it, then there would be no feelings for the spectator to sympathize with; and if no sympathetic feelings then no moral feelings.

Sympathy interests us in the good of mankind; and if sympathy were the source of our esteem for virtue, that sentiment of approbation cou'd only take place, where the virtue actually attain'd its end, and was beneficial to mankind. (*Treatise*, p. 584.)

To this Hume replies that it does not matter whether a quality in an individual achieves its end : the spectator is just as pleased or as pained by it as if it really had. His imagination passes from the cause to the effect, contingent circumstances being no obstacle to this transition. In this the imagination is governed by 'general rules' :

Where a character is, in every respect, fitted to be beneficial to society, the imagination passes easily from the cause to the effect,

[1] My italics.
[2] Hume's position here seems to imply that spontaneous benevolence is not necessarily admirable. This is in apparent contradiction with his earlier acceptance of the 'natural' virtues of benevolence and generosity in their 'confined' and partisan form. (See John Laird, *Hume's Philosophy of Human Nature*, pp. 220-1.)

without considering that there are still some circumstances wanting to render the cause a compleat one. *General rules* create a species of probability, which sometimes influences the judgement, and always the imagination. (*Treatise*, p. 585.)

The implication of Hume's answer is that the spectator will have to sympathize with the hypothetical pain or pleasure of hypothetical associates of the agent or the hypothetical pain or pleasure of the agent himself. Only on such a condition would it be possible for the moral feelings to be aroused in such circumstances. It is obvious that a great deal could be said both about this suggestion and the previous suggestion about the general point of view; but I want to reserve more detailed comment until the following chapter.

Hume finds that the mental qualities or characteristics which through sympathy arouse in the spectator the feelings of moral approval and disapproval do so in two different ways. We are morally pleased or displeased

either from the mere species or appearance of characters and passions or from reflexions on their tendency to the happiness of mankind, and of particular persons. (*Treatise*, p. 589.)

In the first case we are pleased or displeased by qualities which are immediately agreeable either to the agent himself or to his associates. The spectator may sympathize with pleasure or discomfort which a man *himself* derives directly from the possession of some quality; so much so that even though a bad habit or deficiency causes suffering only to the subject he may nevertheless appear disagreeable in the eyes of a spectator 'merely on its account' (*Treatise*, p. 589). The spectator may also sympathize with the immediate pleasure or discomfort which certain qualities (for instance, 'wit, and a certain easy and disengag'd behaviour', *Treatise*, p. 590) cause in a man's *associates*. In so far as we take up an impartial and general point of view we are in a position to see ourselves as others see us; as Hume says: 'A man will be mortified, if you tell him he has a stinking breath; tho' 'tis evidently no annoyance to himself.' (*Treatise*, p. 589.) We take this sympathy with ourselves so far that we become anxious about the kind of impression we are making on complete strangers in whom we have no interest at all. As Hume much earlier remarked, 'the minds of men are mirrors to one another' (*Treatise*, p. 365). But although this first class of qualities is important, Hume is of the opinion that 'reflexions on the tendencies of actions have by far the greatest influence, and determine all the great lines of our duty' (*Treatise*, p. 590). The qualities which are attributed to great men are divided into those which 'make them perform their part in society' (generosity and humanity) and those which 'render them serviceable to themselves, and enable them to promote their own interests' (prudence, temperance, frugality, industry, assiduity, enterprise and dexterity) (*Treatise*, p. 587). Here again, the feelings of approval and disapproval are caused by the spectator's sympathy with the satisfaction or uneasiness felt by the associates of the agent or by the agent himself. In some cases, the 'causes are intermix'd in our judgements of morals' (*Treatise*, p. 590); for example, I may sympathize both with the discomfort a violent cough is causing its owner and with the uneasiness it is causing in those around him. Perhaps the point of greatest interest in this section, though, is the fact that Hume is talking in terms of 'reflection'. He is not absolutely clear as to whether it is the agent or the spectator who does the reflecting; for it would be open for the spectator to sympathize with the pleasure or pain which the agent himself felt on the contemplation of his own talents and failings, as much as it would be for the spectator to reflect on the talents and failings of the agent. But since the first alternative would mean that the morality of a man's conduct would be ultimately determined by his own opinion of it, I think we can discount it and assume that it is the spectator who does the reflecting 'on the tendencies of actions'. Clearly, the point to emphasize is the fact that the 'tendencies' of conduct have now to be taken into consideration in moral judgements. Exactly how this complicates Hume's position I shall leave until the next chapter.

To summarize my account of Hume's position so far. We approve or disapprove of qualities, dispositions, and characteristics (and, but less properly, of the conduct these inspire) in others and ourselves which—when contemplated from a general and disinterested point of view—arouse in us through sympathy certain feelings of pleasure and satisfaction or certain feelings of pain and uneasiness. These qualities are of four kinds: (a) those immediately agreeable to the agent; (b) those immediately agreeable to his associates or society as a whole; (c) those useful to the agent; and (d) those useful to his associates or society as a whole. In so far as approval and disapproval may be considered to be objective variants of the indirect passions and the account of the genesis of the indirect passions the model for the genesis of approval and disapproval, it becomes clear why sympathy has to play such an important part in moral judgement. For one of the causal conditions of the indirect passions is an association of impressions; and in those cases in which he is not directly involved himself it is only through the communicating medium of sympathy that the person who is to feel the moral feeling and make the moral judgement can come to experience the impression necessary if this association of impressions is to take place. But both in our sympathetic reactions and in our direct emotional responses to others we are prejudiced. So in order to avoid the distortion caused by personal involvement we have deliberately to adopt an impartial and general point of view; and from this standpoint sympathize with the feelings of the moral agent himself and/or those affected by his conduct. By this procedure we can even sympathize with the feelings we experience ourselves in response to the agent's conduct; and, the other way about, with the feelings of others in response to our own conduct. In the latter case we can be both agent and spectator. Thus it is possible for us to evaluate those situations in which we are closely involved, either as agent or associate. In some cases this will involve sympathizing with imaginary feelings of imaginary associates. Furthermore, in some, if not all, cases the spectator who makes the moral judgement will be involved in making some kind of judgement as to the utility of certain kinds of disposition and conduct. Although they can be classed as indirect, approval and disapproval are objective passions and as such are to be distinguished from the biased love and hatred, pride and humility. When someone experiences a feeling of moral approval or disapproval this is not to respond immediately to a situation (as it is in the case of the other indirect passions); on the contrary, it is to experience an emotion which on every occasion must be mediated both by sympathy and by the notion of the general point of view.

To conclude this chapter I want to consider two allied though distinct questions. The first is: What is Hume's account of the nature of evaluation? The second is: What analysis of moral language does this account commit Hume to? In so far as these are issues central to Hume's moral philosophy what follows should help to place in a wider context the preceding discussion which has so far centred exclusively around his treatment of sympathy.

In the last chapter of *Passion and Value in Hume's Treatise* Árdal distinguishes between what he calls the Emotionist and Reflectivist interpretations of Hume's account of evaluation. The Emotionist would contend that Hume says that evaluations *are* emotions or feelings and that to make an evaluation is to experience a feeling, whilst the Reflectivist would contend that Hume says that evaluations consist in *judgements* that one has certain emotions or feelings (*P.V.H.T.*, p. 194). We can find evidence supporting both views in the same paragraph. 'To have the sense of virtue, is nothing but to *feel* a satisfaction of a particular kind from the contemplation of a character. The very *feeling* constitutes our praise or admiration' seems to favour the Emotionist interpretation; whilst '. . . but in feeling that it pleases after such a particular manner, we in effect feel that it is virtuous. The case is the same as in our judgments concerning all kinds of beauty, and tastes, and sensations. Our approbation is imply'd in the immediate pleasure they convey to us' (*Treatise*, p. 471) seems to favour the Reflectivist. There is no doubt that Hume is more than a little ambiguous. Árdal eventually comes down on the side of Emotionism. But he adds that a reading of the confused criticism of Hume's doctrines by his contemporary, Thomas Reid, might tend to suggest that eighteenth-century thinkers in general did not discern Reflectivism and Emotionism as two mutually exclusive alternatives (*P.V.H.T.*, p. 210). If this were so then it would account for Hume's apparent vacillation. A second point which tends to explain Hume's ambiguity is that his doctrine of belief tends to assimilate the concepts of judging and thinking to the concept of feeling. If a belief that something is the case is a lively idea or, in other words, an impression, then the belief or judgement that you are experiencing a particular feeling is not going to be distinguishable from the feeling itself.

Now if we accept the Emotionist interpretation (and I cannot see why not) it leaves Hume's position exposed in two ways. The first is that it does not leave room for unjustified approval and disapproval. I should want to disagree with Rachael Kydd who has suggested (*R.C.H.T.*, p. 174) that Hume's account actually allows for a distinction between, on the one hand, *genuine* approval and disapproval and, on the other, *justified* or *right* approval and disapproval. Her account would be as follows. Although I genuinely try to adopt an impartial and general point of view, I may still fail to recognize the influence of my own interests or

I may find it impossible in a particular situation successfully to exclude all reference to myself. In such cases, although what I feel is a genuine feeling of approval, it is not right approval in that it cannot justify the evaluation I make on the strength of it. But although this distinction has a *prima facie* plausibility, if we turn to the text of the *Treatise* we find that Hume thinks that if a feeling of approval or disapproval turns out to be based on a biased view of the situation then it cannot be a feeling of approval or disapproval after all. What we have done is to mistake a feeling of love or liking for one of approval or a feeling of hatred for one of disapproval. This kind of mistake is possible because of the strong relation of resemblance between love and approval and between hatred and disapproval. That the moral feelings are by definition objective is made clear enough at the beginning of Book Three:

'Tis only when a character is consider'd in general, without reference to our particular interest, that it causes such a feeling or sentiment, as denominates it morally good or evil. (*Treatise*, p. 472.)

Objectivity is thus held to be a necessary condition of the moral feelings if they are to count as such. Of course, what Hume is suggesting is not borne out by common experience. If I tell someone that I approve of *X* but during conversation come to realize that in making my judgement I was not objective and was swayed by my own interests, what is the natural thing for me to say? Surely that my approval was unjustified or partisan—but not, what Hume's account suggests, that I had never approved of *X* or that I had mistakenly believed that I had approved of *X*. But although Rachel Kydd's interpretation is more in line with ordinary usage, it is nevertheless mistaken as an interpretation of Hume.

The second difficulty involved in Hume's account of evaluation is the one characteristically associated with the Cartesian psychology I have previously referred to. If approval and disapproval are passions, simple and unanalysable, then they are only contingently connected with conduct. Thus a man may have a feeling of approval or disapproval but this need not commit him to any action or give him a motive for action. In fact, approval and disapproval would be logically compatible with any kind of behaviour. Now if a man constantly asserted that he disapproved of *X* but if, although it were within his power, he consistently did nothing to back up his assertions then we should conclude that he was, according to circumstances, either lying, self-deceived, weak-willed, or that he did not appreciate the meaning of what he was saying. The point is that what a man does is one of the spectator's principal criteria for what he feels. Yet on Hume's account it is only an accident of nature that an attitude of approval should be connected with or accompanied by behaviour designed to favour, encourage, or reward the person who is the object of the approval and that an attitude of disapproval should be connected with or accompanied by behaviour designed to discourage or punish the person who is the object of the disapproval. On Hume's view, it would be perfectly conceivable to encourage attitudes of which you disapproved and to discourage attitudes of which you approved.

We can now come on to the vexed problem of what analysis of evaluative expressions Hume's account of evaluation implies. To be fair to him, we should point out that in the *Treatise* Hume was concerned with giving an account of evaluation itself rather than evaluative language. The consequence of this is that the field has been left open for several different interpretations. Árdal distinguishes three schools of thought. Thus Hume has been credited with the views that evaluative utterances: (a) make statements about the speaker's feelings (Subjectivism); (b) make statements about other people's feelings (C. D. Broad's interpretation in *Five Types of Ethical Theory*); and (c) express in some sense the speaker's feelings (Emotivism). Árdal rejects interpretations (a) and (b) (although he admits that in some places Hume, for various reasons, writes as if he were advocating some kind of Subjectivism) and inclines cautiously to the view that the analysis of moral language which is most in keeping with Hume's general philosophical position is Emotivism.

It seems to me that Árdal is perfectly justified in dismissing Broad's analysis[1] as inadequate. In the latter's view, 'for Hume the statement "X is good" *means* the same as the statement "X is such that the contemplation of it would call forth an emotion of approval towards it in all or most men."' (*F.T.E.T.*, p. 85.) With this as his premise Broad goes on to make the criticism that the logical conclusion of Hume's analysis is that in ethical disputes, far from there coming a stage beyond which one could only say

[1] For similar interpretations see A. H. Basson, *David Hume*, pp. 103–4; Basil Willey, *The Eighteenth-Century Background*, p. 119.

de gustibus non est disputandum, there is always a method by which one could reach agreement: all that would be required would be to make observations and collect statistics of people's actual approvals and disapprovals; moral dilemmas would be capable of resolution by social surveys (*F.T.E.T.*, p. 115). No doubt Broad is right in complaining that an ethical theory which equates what is good with what most people think is good is woefully inadequate; but there is no doubt equally that he is wrong in supposing that this is the theory Hume is advocating. Broad bases his views exclusively on the *Enquiry Concerning the Principles of Morals* ('the best account of Hume's theory of ethics', *F.T.E.T.*, p. 84); but since he does not give a single reference it is not clear what led him to make such a misleading interpretation. It is possible, though, that Hume's restricted concept of approval has caused Hume to write sometimes as if 'what is actually approved' is equivalent to 'what should be approved'; and that this has influenced Broad's alleged analysis. According to Hume, approval is necessarily objective and there is no room in his concept for the possibility of 'unjustified approval'. There is no logical gap between my feeling approval of X and X being good; moreover, X would still be good even if as a matter of fact I was the only person to approve of it. The point is that for Hume, although it is possible not to recognize what is good as good, it is impossible to approve of that which is not good; and it is fairly clear from his analysis that Broad has failed to appreciate this. I shall presently suggest what I think is a more viable alternative to Broad's analysis.

Whilst agreeing in principle with Árdal's opinion of Broad's analysis, it seems to me that there are a few points in the context of Árdal's treatment of the Subjectivist interpretation which can be profitably discussed. First, I had better put Árdal's position more fully. To exemplify the Subjectivist point of view Árdal quotes the following passage from an article by Geoffrey Hunter:

Hume's analysis of moral arguments is mistaken. For, among other things, it has the consequence that if one person says of an action that it is wholly virtuous and another person says of the same action that it is wholly vicious, these two people would not be contradicting each other, since one is saying the logical equivalent of 'I [Smith] feel a peculiar sort of pleasure, and I do not feel a peculiar sort of pain, on contemplating this action', while the other is saying the equivalent of 'I [Jones] feel a peculiar sort of pain, and I do not feel a peculiar sort of pleasure, on contemplating this action', and both these statements could be true. If they were both true, and Hume's analysis were correct, then one and the same action would *be* both wholly virtuous and wholly vicious, which, in the ordinary senses of the words used, is absurd. ('Hume on "Is" and "Ought"', *Philosophy* (1962), pp. 151–2.)

That is, such statements as 'X is virtuous' and 'X is vicious' are to be taken as statements about the speaker's feelings; from this it follows that the truth of such statements depends upon who makes them. Now Árdal rejects this as an interpretation of Hume's position on two grounds.[1] (a) No good explanation has been advanced (by Hunter or anyone else) for why Hume should have held a view with so little to recommend it (*P.V.H.T.*, p. 200). (b) If we want to credit Hume with Emotionism as a doctrine about the nature of evaluations themselves, then to suppose that he was putting forward Subjectivism as a doctrine about the nature of evaluative language, although logically feasible, would mean the loss of the ordinary-language distinction between openly evaluating and talking about one's evaluations or, in other words, making second-order statements, as one would, say, to a psychiatrist (*P.V.H.T.*, pp. 195–7). Two explanations as to why Hume should have written in some places as if he were advocating some kind of Subjectivism are suggested (cf. the explanations for Hume's apparent Reflectivism).

(a) Hume did not clearly distinguish between the meaning of a sentence and a description of the conditions which justify its use on a particular occasion. Thus in the following important passage from the first section of Book Three:

> . . . when you pronounce any action or character to be vicious, you mean nothing, but that from the constitution of your own nature you have a feeling or sentiment of blame from the contemplation of it. (*Treatise*, p. 469.)

Hume could be understood as giving the linguistic equivalent of the sentence 'X is vicious'. This would be the Subjectivist reading. But equally he could be understood as characterising

---

[1] Although it does not affect the points here under discussion, in order to avoid unnecessary confusion it is worth mentioning that there is a fallacy in Hunter's argument as it is presented in this extract. It does *not*, in fact, follow from the alleged analysis that 'the same action would be wholly virtuous and wholly vicious'. Hunter subsequently withdrew this part of his thesis (see 'A Reply to Professor Flew', *Philosophy* (1963)).

the conditions which entitle you to say 'X is vicious'; in other words, as saying that the feeling of disapproval justifies the utterance 'X is vicious'. Thus although the fact that I say 'X is vicious' implies that I have (or think I have) a feeling of disapproval on the contemplation of X, to say 'X is vicious' is not to say 'I have a feeling of disapproval on the contemplation of X' (*P.V.H.T.*, pp. 205–6). (b) In so far as his theory of belief tends to assimilate thinking to feeling, the distinction between having a feeling and judging that you have a feeling will be, to Hume, blurred (*P.V.H.T.*, p. 210). Compared with Subjectivism as a doctrine about the function of moral language, Emotivism would preserve the distinction between evaluating and reflecting upon one's evaluations. Árdal concludes:

> Although one can, with some confidence, call Hume an Emotionist, one cannot attribute Emotivism to him with equal degree of certainty. Hume's sentimentalist account of thinking fits in well with an expressive, non-propositional analysis of evaluative utterances. It would in general, fit in well with Hume's associationist scheme when this is applied to the explanation of our use of language. But in attributing Emotivism to Hume, one is not directly interpreting his words, but rather considering what position would be most in conformity with other aspects of his philosophy. (*P.V.H.T.*, p. 212.)

Now in the first place I want to draw attention to a certain implication which Hume's doctrine of approval and disapproval has in this context. Árdal argues that given the Subjectivist analysis it must follow that the meanings of such statements as 'X is virtuous' and 'X is vicious' will vary systematically from speaker to speaker (*P.V.H.T.*, p. 199). However, if we bear in mind what Hume has said about approval and disapproval this conclusion does not follow. It does not follow that to construe 'X is virtuous' as 'I have a feeling of approval on the contemplation of X' and 'X is vicious' as 'I have a feeling of disapproval on the contemplation of X' will lead to the paradoxical situation where Smith may say that X is virtuous and Jones that X is vicious and yet neither be contradicting the other. On the contrary, once the non-ethical factors had been cleared up to each party's satisfaction (assuming that possibility), then if Smith and Jones were still maintaining their verbally conflicting positions it would have to follow that at least one of them was not after all experiencing a genuine feeling of (as the case may be) approval or disapproval. This has to follow because, according to Hume, approval and disapproval are necessarily based on an impartial and general contemplation of persons and their actions; and since this is by definition a viewpoint from which *everyone* would have to agree if placed in it, there can be no room for a situation where one person approves of X whilst another disapproves, or vice versa. Ultimately, then, Hume commits himself to the position of denying the possibility of real moral disagreement.

If what I have said is correct then it leads to the following interesting implication to do with the method of verification of such evaluative expressions as 'X is virtuous' and 'X is vicious'. If I want to verify Smith's statement that X is virtuous then there are several ways of going about this. I may consider to what extent Smith occupies an impartial standpoint in relation to X and, if not, to what extent Smith is capable of abstracting himself from his own contingent circumstances and achieving some measure of objectivity. In this way, then, I should be concentrating attention on the reliability of the speaker. But there are alternative methods at my disposal: I can consult either my own feelings towards X or other people's feelings towards X. At this point the distinction which Árdal mentions between the meaning of a sentence and the conditions of its use is very helpful. Following Árdal, we can say that for Hume the passage beginning 'When you pronounce . . .' (*Treatise*, p. 469) gives the conditions for the use of such expressions as 'X is virtuous' and 'X is vicious'. But it does not seem to me that we must go on from this to attribute to Hume an Emotivist theory of the function of moral language. I would suggest that for Hume such an expression as 'X is virtuous' could be understood as equivalent to 'X is such that an impartial spectator contemplating it would experience a certain feeling of pleasure towards it' or, more briefly, 'X is an object of approval' (cf. Broad's analysis). To say this would be consistent with the view that 'I have a feeling of approval towards X' refers to the condition which justifies my use in this particular context of the evaluating expression 'X is virtuous'; for although whenever I say 'X is virtuous' I can also say 'I have a feeling of approval towards X', the latter is not what I *mean* when I say 'X is virtuous'. The analysis I am suggesting would, moreover, still have the advantage of preserving the distinction between openly evaluating and talking about one's evaluations. When I say 'I have a feeling of approval (or disapproval) towards X' there would be no doubt that I was drawing attention to my feelings themselves and not passing judgement on X.[1]

It scarcely needs pointing out that no really hard-and-fast conclusions emerge from this discussion. If it is probable that Hume's philosophy contains a latent Emotivist streak, it is equally as probable that the analysis which I have suggested in terms of the feelings of the objective spectator is correct. I am not thoroughly convinced by either the Subjectivist or the Emotivist interpretations. Subjectivism is such an inherently implausible position to have to adopt; and one cannot help feeling that Emotivism has gained a victory in Árdal's view largely through default of the only other contender. As Árdal admits, there is virtually no direct evidence in the *Treatise* for the Emotivist interpretation. Having introduced what I hope is a viable alternative to both Emotivism and Subjectivism as theories about the function of moral language, I shall leave the topic here. My intention has been to place the doctrine of sympathy as the medium of moral judgement in a wider context. In the following chapter I want to pick up some loose ends which have periodically appeared in this one and especially to discuss the relation between feeling and reason which this doctrine implies.

[1] This analysis would also fit in with Hunter's contention that in the famous 'is-ought' passage (*Treatise*, p. 469) what Hume is doing is complaining that previous philosophers have failed adequately to explain how one can move from a statement of fact to one of value and *not*, as is often thought, denying this possibility altogether. For the various ramifications of the 'is-ought' controversy see the collection *The Is-Ought Question*, edited by W. D. Hudson (London 1969).

IV

REASON AND SYMPATHY IN
THE *TREATISE*

THIS chapter will be devoted to the study of the role of 'reason' in Hume's sympathetic theory of moral judgement. The whole undertaking of tying sympathy to morality involves two great difficulties. The first is that sympathy is both capricious and partial. Hume's solution to this problem is explicitly developed in the idea of sympathizing from a general, disinterested point of view. The second is that sympathy is blind to value. Hume does not deal with this problem as such and I shall presently discuss what answer his account implies. Broadly speaking, though, the only way in which both these problems are to be overcome is by injecting into the account an element of reasoning or reflection of some kind. This is, in fact, the course which Hume, more or less surreptitiously, takes. The first question I therefore want to discuss is: To what extent is it true that the viability of Hume's sympathetic theory of evaluation depends upon the introduction of some kind of reasoning or reflection? But Hume's well-known derogation of the powers of reason in contrast to those of the passions creates the further question: To what extent is the role to which reason must be delegated in the sympathetic theory consistent with what Hume says elsewhere about the powers of reason? Clearly, we shall have to decide just what limits Hume does propose to set on the powers of reason in relation to those of the passions. It has been suggested that Hume's philosophy lacks a genuine concept of practical reason: the following discussion will have some bearing on this criticism.

We have seen that a vital part of Hume's account of evaluation is that we are able to 'correct' our immediate attitudes and opinions. If we are to feel genuine approval and disapproval we must possess an adequate idea of the object of our approval or disapproval: if we do not possess this adequate idea then our feelings, whatever else they may be, cannot be counted as moral feelings. The question whether my feeling of approval or disapproval is justified or not just cannot arise. I have used the deliberately vague term 'adequate idea' because Hume does not express himself very clearly on this point. He insists that in moral judgement the spectator must adopt a general point of view; but he does not go to much trouble to explain exactly what is involved in doing this. What he does suggest is that the spectator must contemplate the other person and his conduct in such a way as to exclude all reference to his own (accidental) circumstances, especially his own interests. If each one of us looked at and evaluated every situation from his own particular point of view the result would be chaos. To avoid this, we deliberately seek out an impartial point of view, and endeavour to judge each situation from this standpoint, no matter how much our own personal interests and feelings are involved. Although our immediate sentiments of praise and blame may be 'corrected' through the adoption of the general reference point, in practice this does not always happen. In practice we are too bound up with ourselves to become involved with matters which do not promise us some kind of benefit or to be able to judge fairly someone whose interests conflict with our own.

> Here we are contented with saying, that reason requires such an impartial conduct, but that 'tis seldom that we can bring ourselves to it, and that our passions do not readily follow the determination of our judgment. (*Treatise*, p. 583.)

Now, on the face of it, for Hume to talk about the passions as following or not following the determination of our judgement does seem out of character. But he explains that by 'reason' or 'judgment' here we must understand 'a general calm determination of the passions, founded on some distant view or reflexion'. It is in this sense that we should think of 'reason' as 'opposing' the passions. In so far as to 'correct' one's feelings through the adoption of the general point of view results in a 'general calm determination of the passions, founded on some distant view or reflexion', the feelings of the agent who does adopt this standpoint may legitimately be said to be 'reasonable'.

But there is no doubt that there is more involved in the idea of sympathizing from a general point of view (even in the restricted sense so far mentioned) than Hume admits. To begin with, it implies that the spectator has to adopt a standpoint other than the one he happens to occupy at the time; and to attempt to adopt a standpoint of any description must involve deliberation and reflection. It assumes in the agent the ability to put himself in others' shoes (which in turn seems to depend upon the capacity for some kind of sympathetic understanding of others). I think that we could say that to sympathize from a general point of view is equivalent to *knowing how one would feel if one were impartial.* This comes out in, for instance, the following passage:

> We blame equally a bad action, which we read of in history, with one perform'd in our neighbourhood t'other day: The meaning of which is, that we know from reflexion, that the former action wou'd excite as strong sentiments of disapprobation [in us] as the latter, were it plac'd in the same position. (*Treatise*, p. 584, cf. p. 482.)

Hume tends to slide over the differences between unmediated sympathy and this mediated sympathy as if the difference were one of degree rather than of kind. But the difference is the difference between actually having a sympathetic feeling in a particular situation and imagining what sympathetic feeling we would have if the situation were changed in a particular respect: the first is a purely affective process (at least in Hume's sense of 'sympathy') whilst the second is a reflective one.

So far we have only been considering the spectator's accidental circumstances. But it is necessary to take into account the agent's circumstances. Virtue in rags is still virtue. If a man is in prison then his instinctive generosity will be frustrated; and this will mean that there are in existence no feelings of satisfaction or pleasure for the spectator to sympathize with and hence no possibility for approval. What therefore the spectator has to do is to view the situation in general terms; he must look at the agent's qualities out of context. In short, he must concentrate on what feelings *would be felt if things were different.* Here also it seems clear that no matter how habitual this way of looking at things becomes it is a fundamentally thoughtful procedure. It is worth noting that in this kind of case (where the agent's qualities are frustrated) the inadequacy of the spectator's ideas would result not in biased sympathy but in no sympathy at all.

Now in the sense mentioned so far, to adopt a general viewpoint is an antidote to the lack of principle which sympathy displays. But to exclude reference to ourself is not in itself enough to enable us to form an adequate idea of the situation under consideration. It is not enough to be able to sympathize impartially with someone else's pleasure or pain: we must also know whether this pain or pleasure has any value beyond itself. But sympathy and value are logically independent of each other: I may sympathize with someone whose feelings and behaviour I recognize to be utterly without value to himself or others. But this creates a dilemma; since according to Hume's observations what all virtuous behaviour has in common is that it is either useful or agreeable to the agent himself and/or his associates. The only way out of this dilemma is to say that the spectator who makes the moral judgement will also have to make some judgement as to the utility of the conduct or quality under consideration. This means that he cannot rely merely on his feelings. *Per se*, pleasure is agreeable and pain disagreeable; but there may be factors in a particular situation which alter this correspondence. The only way to discover whether this is the case is to inspect the situation. Suppose that I see A stopping B from doing something which it is obvious to me that B very much wants to do. I may sympathize with B's frustration and misery and this sympathy (on the theory up to now, so long as I have excluded reference to myself) will cause me to disapprove of A's conduct. But on deeper investigation I may find that appearances are deceptive and perhaps either that A did not realize he was causing B pain or that he did realize but was aiming at B's long-term happiness (say, the case of a father withholding his consent from what he thought to be an unsuitable marriage) or that he did realize but was aiming at other people's benefit or even the long-term benefit of the community (say, in the case of punishment). On being in full possession of the facts my disapproval of A may turn to approval. If this did happen, then my approval of A would be perfectly compatible with my immediate sympathy with B's pain. Now it should be clear from this that it is not just a case of sympathizing with the feelings of the agent and/or those affected by his conduct together with the adoption of a neutral point of view—evaluation must *also* involve the recognition of the true interests of the people concerned. As I have said, Hume goes to little trouble to confirm this; the vagueness of the following passage is typical:

When any quality, or character, has a tendency to the good of mankind, we are pleas'd with it, and approve of it; because it presents the lively idea of pleasure; which idea affects us by sympathy, and is itself a kind of pleasure. (*Treatise*, p. 580.)

Although Hume perpetually refers to the 'general view of things' (*Treatise*, p. 587) or the 'common point of view' (*Treatise*, p. 591), nowhere does he really satisfactorily unpack this notion. It seems to me that it might be possible to interpret it not only as involving the exclusion of the spectator's contingent circumstances but also as involving the consideration and balancing of the interests of the agent, his associates and the community as a whole. This comes out in one passage in particular (the conclusion of the first section of Book Three) where Hume specifically mentions the 'interests' as well as the feelings of the agent and his associates:

. . . every particular person's pleasure and interest being different, 'tis impossible men cou'd ever agree in their sentiments and judgments, unless they chose some common point of view, from which they might survey their object, and which might cause it to appear the same to all of them. Now, in judging of characters, the only interest or pleasure, which appears the same to every spectator, is that of the person himself, whose character is examin'd; or that of persons, who have a connexion with him. And tho' such interests and pleasures touch us more faintly than our own, yet being more constant and universal, they counter-ballance the latter even in practice, and are alone admitted in speculation as the standard of virtue and morality. They alone produce that particular feeling or sentiment, on which moral distinctions depend. (*Treatise*, p. 591.)

From what Hume says here it is not clear whether he would be thinking in terms of act or rule utilitarianism; that is, whether an action should be considered as having certain consequences in itself or whether it should be considered as falling under a class of actions which, as a class, has certain consequences. Hume's insistence that it is mental qualities or dispositions rather than actions which are the proper objects of moral judgement (*Treatise*, p. 575) may suggest that rule utilitarianism is most in keeping with Hume's general position. However, from the point of view of what follows it is does not really matter which is the case.

Now, with reference to the above passage, it is clear how the satisfaction or uneasiness of the agent and his associates can, through sympathy, 'produce that particular feeling or sentiment, on which moral distinctions depend'; but what is not so clear is exactly how the interests of the agent and/or his associates may be 'admitted in speculation as the standard of virtue and morality'. The spectator cannot sympathize with these interests; for, in Hume's sense, sympathy is exclusively the communication of feelings. There is no other alternative but to conclude that the spectator's comprehensive utility judgement is in some sense capable of exerting an influence on his feelings of sympathy. To go back to the example: my approval of A's conduct cannot rest solely on the belief that it will benefit B and/or the community as a whole or on the belief that it falls into a class of acts which has effects beneficial to individuals in B's position and/or to the community as a whole; for the essence of Hume's position is that approval (and disapproval) is not caused by beliefs of this kind but by the spectator's sympathetic feeling. If he is to feel approval, the spectator must sympathize with a feeling of satisfaction then; but the awkward question arises as to *whose* feeling this will be. Is it the feeling of pleasure that B would experience on realizing that A after all had had his interests at heart? But B may never realize this. And even if he does recognize A's good intentions this need not alleviate his misery at the time or afford him any satisfaction in retrospect. The spectator's assumption must nevertheless be that B would feel pleased if he knew the full facts of the situation; if, that is, he knew the direction of his own real interests together with what A's real motives were. In so far as the spectator is to evaluate A's conduct he will have to pay attention to this hypothetical reaction from B: what he judges this to be will depend upon the outcome of his comprehensive utility judgement. How the spectator decides the utility question will determine whether B's real feelings or the feelings he imagines would be B's turn out to be the object of his sympathy. We can call this judgement a 'practical empirical judgement'. It is 'practical' because the whole point of its being made is to influence the feelings of the person who makes it.

This dependence on some kind of reflection is especially apparent in Hume's account of the 'artificial' virtues (justice, promise-keeping, respect for property, and chastity). Hume locates the principal difference between a natural virtue and an artificial virtue in the fact that naturally virtuous acts have immediately beneficial consequences whilst artificially virtuous acts need not necessarily. The value of the artificial virtues is to be found not so much in the consequences of individual acts as in the consequences of upholding the particular institutions and customs themselves. A particular act may be a just act but for all that it need not do any individual any good and it may do someone a great deal of harm. This account immediately lands the sympathetic theory in its simple form in a difficulty. The sympathetic theory requires that the spectator sympathize with the feelings of the agent and or his associates. But if the unjust act is not necessarily injurious to any individual and is potentially the source of more immediate good than immediate harm (say, in the case of the judge who deliberately misinterprets the law in favour of the poor and underprivileged), then it is hard to see how in such a case there would be any feelings of uneasiness for the spectator to sympathize with. Hume characteristically glosses over the problem; for instance:

> . . . when the injustice is so distant from us, as no way to affect our interest, it still displeases us; because we consider it as prejudicial to human society, and pernicious to everyone that approaches the person guilty of it. We partake of their uneasiness by *sympathy*. . . . (*Treatise*, p. 499.)

But if the unjust act is not necessarily damaging to anyone, how can it be the case that it is 'pernicious to everyone that approaches the person guilty of it'? If the spectator is to sympathize with the uneasiness of all those in contact with the unjust man then it must follow either that these people have already condemned the man and Hume is begging the question or that the spectator has recognized, independently of his feelings, that justice is an institution useful to the community as a whole and on the basis of this judgement has assumed that the response of the agent's associates will be one of uneasiness. The key phrase seems to be 'because we *consider* it prejudicial to human society'. It is the spectator's recognition of what is in the 'public interest' (*Treatise*, p. 500) which determines what the object of his sympathy will be. Telescoping his argument, Hume even talks about a 'sympathy with public interest'—a phrase which on his definition of 'sympathy' is absurd. Without this appeal to the spectator's capacity for reasoning Hume's account of the artificial virtues could not make sense.

There are therefore three ways in which my idea of a situation may, from a moral point of view, be inadequate: (a) if I fail to exclude the influence of my own contingent circumstances; (b) if I am misled by the particular circumstances of the other person; and (c) if I fail to make (or make a wrong) comprehensive utility judgement about the conduct and character of the person under consideration. Of these, (a) and (c) are by far the most important.

Finally, there is just one more further factor 'which the spectator has to take into account when he makes a moral judgement; that is, whether the agent has any special duties or responsibilities or commitments. About this Hume says:

> . . . we always consider the *natural* and *usual* force of the passions, when we determine concerning vice and virtue; and if the passions depart very much from the common measures on either side, they are always disapprov'd as vicious. A man naturally loves his children better than his nephews, his nephews better than his cousins, his cousins better than strangers, where every thing else is equal. Hence arise our common measures of duty, in preferring the one to the other. Our sense of duty always follows the common and natural course of our passions. (*Treatise*, p. 483.)

Particular relations between individuals (for instance, those between one friend and another, a parent and a child, etc.) give rise to characteristic 'duties'. The nature of these 'duties' is determined by social custom. In carrying them out, if we 'depart very much from the common measures', if, that is, we do the unexpected and step outside the socially accepted limits of behaviour, then our conduct must be condemned as vicious and intolerable. It is this kind of statement which has earned Hume a bad reputation and prompted several critics to condemn Hume as a mere advocate of an ethic of respectability. Of recent examples, I am thinking in particular of Dorothea Krook's scathing attack in *Three Traditions of Moral Thought* (pp. 176–7). This subject opens up many extremely interesting ideas; but I shall restrict myself to the following brief observations. (a) As a representation of the whole of Hume's moral philosophy this kind of criticism is very misleading. Only if we suppose that the spectator's sympathy is unmediated by a utility judgement such as I have suggested is it reasonable to conclude that Hume is advocating an ethic of respectability. For instance, in the case of self-evaluation it is a mistake to imagine that Hume's account implies that if others think well of us we shall necessarily approve of ourselves. This would only follow if we supposed that those whom my conduct affects, and with whom, in order to evaluate my own conduct, I have to sympathize, recognize their true long-term interests. Of course, it is a different matter if someone else genuinely approves or disapproves of me; for on Hume's account this would mean that I should have to approve or disapprove of myself, as the case may be. But we should remember that on Hume's definition approval must be strictly distinguished from mere liking, love, flattery, or popularity. (b) However, we have to admit there is more than a grain of truth in this criticism of Hume. Of an urbane and equable temperament, he had little sympathy with the enthusiast or extremist of any sort. The range of values to which he draws attention in the *Treatise* reflects the undeniable parochialism of his own moral outlook. The fact remains, though, that the boundaries of respectability expand or shrink from society to society; and although Hume did not consciously make provision for this fact his theory nevertheless seems capable of accommodating it without much upheaval. (c) It is arguable that the kind of conduct which conforms with social expectation is based ultimately on social utility. Customs, habits, and traditions are essential to any society; for without them it would lose its identity. Likewise, the stability of a society must to some extent depend on the conservatism of its members. But it seems doubtful whether these facts can ever justify making 'departure from the common measures' *per se* a moral issue. In any case, Hume grossly oversimplifies: the fact that a man does not love his children does not make him an object of moral condemnation in the same way that his betrayal of a friend's trust would. This illustrates Hume's general tendency to spread the moral net wide and rather indiscriminately. (d) Finally, to return to the main theme of this chapter, it is clear that in specifying this further condition about the 'natural and usual force of the passions' Hume is asking that the spectator of the moral situation should do some kind of reflecting on that situation.

Now at first sight the active role which I have allotted to reasoning or reflection in the sympathetic theory of moral judgement does not tally with what Hume says elsewhere about the powers of 'reason'. It seems to me that the whole point of a spectator's adoption of a general point of view must be to arouse within him (through the medium of sympathy) the feelings of approval and disapproval in accordance with which moral judgements are made. If he reflects as to what his feelings would be if he were truly disinterested then the outcome of this reflection has to be a judgement which commits him to having certain moral feelings and consequently to doing certain things. If the spectator reflects on the utility (both for the agent himself and the community as a whole) of particular acts and certain kinds of behaviour (and their corresponding mental qualities) then the judgements which are the outcome of these reflections must be practical in that they commit the spectator to certain feelings of approval or disapproval. How then is it possible to reconcile the fact that the sympathy theory seems to draw upon some concept of practical reason with the reason-as-the-slave-of-the-passions theme which is so prominent in Book Three?

In this context it is the opening section of Book Three which usually receives most attention. There, Hume dismisses in a paragraph the various contemporary brands of rationalist moral thinking (*Treatise*, p. 456). The mistake which they all share is the claim that the content of morality can be discovered through thought alone. It is Hume's view on the contrary that morality is essentially grounded in human nature and that there can be no such thing as moral good and evil independent of human nature. He emphatically denies the possibility of practical *a priori* truths— the possibility, that is, of 'eternal fitnesses and unfitnesses of things, which are the same to every rational being that considers them'. His basic argument in support of this view is that morality being a practical affair (common experience confirms this for us) and reason being by itself wholly inactive, it follows that morality cannot be a function of reason:

Since morals, therefore, have an influence on the actions and affections, it follows, that they cannot be deriv'd from reason; and that because reason alone, as we have already prov'd, can never have any such influence. Morals excite passions, and produce or prevent actions. Reason of itself is utterly impotent in this particular. The rules of morality, therefore, are not conclusions of our reason. (*Treatise*, p. 457.)

Reason or the understanding carries out two functions: the comparing of ideas and the inferring of matters of fact. If it is correct to think of vice and virtue as objects of reason they must fall into one or other of these categories. Hume goes to great pains to show that there cannot possibly be any relation 'susceptible of certainty and demonstration' in which vice and virtue could consist (*Treatise*, pp. 463–8). Just as surely, vice and virtue cannot be matters of fact: in, for instance, a case of murder, although you can discover 'certain passions, motives, volitions, and thoughts' you cannot discover any matter of fact which you could call 'the vice' (*Treatise*, pp. 468–9). It must therefore be improper to describe our actions and emotions as true or false, reasonable or unreasonable.

Reason is the discovery of truth or falshood. Truth or falshood consists in an agreement or disagreement either to the *real* relations of ideas, or to *real* existence and matter of fact. . . . Now 'tis evident our passions, volitions, and actions, are not susceptible of any such agreement or disagreement; being original facts and realities, compleat in themselves, and implying no reference to other passions, volitions, and actions. 'Tis impossible, therefore, they can be pronounced either true or false, and be either contrary or conformable to reason.

. . . Laudable or blameable, therefore, are not the same with reasonable or unreasonable. The merit and demerit of actions frequently contradict, and sometimes controul our natural propensities. But reason has no such influence. Moral distinctions, therefore, are not the offspring of reason. Reason is wholly inactive, and can never be the source of so active a principle as conscience, or a sense of morals. (*Treatise*, p. 458.)

The concept of reason put forward in this section appears, then, to be a very restricted one. But the point we must remember is that in this context Hume has been principally concerned to refute the contemporary rationalists' theories and that his rather dogmatic and epigrammatic style has tended to obscure his more positive concept of reason. Add to this the fact that Hume nowhere explicitly develops this positive side of his thought and it is not surprising that a casual reading of the *Treatise* should leave one with the impression that Hume sees reason as utterly inactive and incapable of influencing behaviour. However, if we look again at the text we shall see that certain statements have been very carefully qualified; for example:

Reason *of itself* is utterly impotent.

. . . 'tis vain to pretend, that morality is discover'd *only* by a deduction of reason.

In order, therefore, to judge of these systems, we need only consider, whether it be possible, from reason *alone*. . . .[1] (*Treatise*, p. 457.)

And in fact, Hume does specifically allow reason to influence conduct in two ways; namely:

Either when it excites a passion by informing us of the existence of something which is a proper object of it; or when it discovers the connexions of causes and effects, so as to afford us means of exerting any passion. (*Treatise*, p. 459.)

Reason can be said to influence conduct in the first way in so far as it can inform us of the existence of an object or objects which

---

[1] My italics.

we already desire. We can term this kind of judgement 'promptive'. An example would be expressed by the statement 'This
apple is sweet and juicy.' In so far as I already possess a desire
for a sweet and juicy apple the judgement that this object before
me is a sweet and juicy apple will prompt this desire. An example
of the second kind of judgement ('directive') would be expressed
by the following statement: 'If I catch the "Cambrian Coast
Express" I shall arrive in Aberystwyth by five o'clock.' This is
a means–ends judgement: if I desire the end it shows me what
I must do to realize this desire. Both of these judgements only
incidentally affect my conduct: the judgement that this is a sweet
and juicy apple is only going to affect my conduct if I already
happen to have a desire for such an apple; and the judgement
that if I catch the 'Cambrian Coast' I shall be in Aberystwyth by
five o'clock will likewise only affect my conduct if I already happen to want to get to Aberystwyth by five o'clock. The judgements themselves do not *cause* my actions. In both kinds of
judgement there is room for mistakes to be made. I may be such
a bad judge of fruit that my apple turns out to be sour and
maggoty. Or I may not realize that British Rail has revised its
timetables so that the 'Cambrian Coast' no longer arrives by five
o'clock. In these cases I may legitimately be said to be acting
'unreasonably'. But there is no question of attaching moral blame
to my actions: I may be stupid but not vicious.

> Reason and judgment may, indeed, be the mediate cause of an
> action, by prompting, or by directing a passion: But it is not pretended,
> that a judgment of this kind, either in its truth or falshood, is attended
> with virtue or vice. (*Treatise*, p. 462.)

We could call this the doctrine of reason as the *mediate cause* of
action. It might be thought that if reason can be held to 'prompt'
an action then this is no different from holding that reason can
'cause' an action by itself. Rachael Kydd points out (*R.C.H.T.*,
pp. 104 f.), in defence of Hume, that it is not the judgement itself
that causes the action or desire but the idea contained in the
judgement. Thus the judgement that this is a sweet and juicy
apple before me brings before the mind the idea of (strictly, my
eating) a sweet and juicy apple; which idea causes a desire to
eat the apple—a desire which had previously not been in existence.
Once the idea is before my mind it is my instincts and dispositions
which determine whether or not a desire will be aroused—not

my reason or understanding. On Hume's account, desires are passions and as such are caused by impressions or ideas. A desire to do X is caused by the thought of X as something which will be accompanied by pleasant sensations (although there are a few exceptions to this rule, for instance, hunger, lust, and revenge). Therefore, Hume is perfectly consistent in maintaining that reason cannot directly cause actions, or desires to do actions, or ideas to arouse desires to do actions. Whether or not an idea gives rise to a desire depends solely on one's instinctive dispositions. On the other hand, reason may, both by drawing attention to the connection between a desired end and a particular action and by making one aware of the possibility of a particular action, influence, albeit indirectly or mediately, one's desires and actions.

Rachael Kydd suggests that a positive concept of practical reason is clearly discernible in the *Treatise* (*R.C.H.T.*, pp. 99–138). Briefly, the position she attributes to Hume is as follows. If we distinguish between *a priori* or demonstrative reasoning and empirical reasoning then Hume admits the possibility of *a priori* judgements incidentally affecting conduct but he denies the possibility of *a priori* practical reasoning. As for empirical reasoning, Hume allows that empirical judgements can incidentally affect conduct in the two ways which I have just examined. But what is particularly interesting in this context is that she goes on to contend that Hume, by implication, admits the possibility of practical empirical judgements or, in other words, judgements which cannot be made without containing implications for what the maker of the judgement does. As with the theoretical empirical judgements which incidentally affect conduct, these practical judgements can be divided into promptive and directive: the possibility of the former is to be inferred from the notion of the calm passions and the possibility of the latter from the account of the artificial virtues. A practical promptive judgement would be about what it would be necessary for me to do in view of the intrinsic nature of the actions open to me and in view of my instinctive dispositions: such would be the judgement made in response to the question 'Do I really want to do X?' In so far as he talks about calm passions which are founded on a 'distant view and reflexion' (*Treatise*, p. 583) Hume should admit the existence of practical promptive judgements. For to found a passion on a distant view and reflection would seem to amount to the same thing as founding a passion on a judgement made as a result of asking ourselves whether in view of its intrinsic nature this is the kind of passion we must have. Although we are often governed by violent passions, 'the calm ones, when corroborated by reflection, and seconded by resolution, are able to controul them in their most furious movements' (*Treatise*, pp. 437–8). To corroborate a passion by reflection must involve asking oneself whether the idea which is the cause of the passion is adequate to its object (that is, undistorted by contingent circumstances) or, in other words, whether this is the passion one must have on reflection. Likewise, our desires to keep promises, respect property, and obey the law are the products of practical judgements; but in these cases they are directive, means–ends judgements. The end which we instinctively desire is a state of peace and security. This can only be achieved through society; and in order to live in society we have to behave in ways to which we are not 'naturally' inclined. Our motives for behaving in these 'artificial' ways cannot be explained in terms of our natural dispositions unaided by reason. But Hume is careful to say that reason cannot give rise to any motive by itself (*Treatise*, p. 496). These means–ends judgements carry with them the force of necessity. We do not merely judge that respecting others' property is a means to conserving our own, but further that in view of this fact we are obliged to respect their property. Hume's arguments commit him to the view that there can be practical judgements about the necessity of adopting the means in view of the desired end. If this interpretation is correct then Hume should have admitted the possibility of a third way of acting 'unreasonably', namely, failure to realize that in view of the fact that X is a means to Y it is necessary to do X.

If we can accept Rachael Kydd's thesis then this shows that it would not be out of character to attribute to Hume a theory which presupposed the possibility of practical judgements. However, if we look again at the kinds of judgements shown to be implicit in the sympathy theory of moral judgement they do not appear to be truly practical. The judgements which are made as results of such questions as 'What feelings would I have towards X if I were truly disinterested?' and 'To what extent is X of benefit to Smith and/or the community in general?' do not in fact commit the maker to any particular feelings or actions. These judgements are theoretical rather than practical; that is, although they may affect feelings and actions, they need not. That these judgements are only theoretical is in contradiction, though, with what I said earlier in this chapter where I suggested that the judgements which are implicit in the sympathy theory must be practical if the theory is to be made viable. This contradiction can be seen as a reflection of the intractability of Hume's material. Moral evaluation is in accordance with certain feelings which are aroused through sympathy. In order to fulfil its mediating role, sympathy need only be thought of as a transition of feeling from one person to another. In this sense, sympathy is characterized by an intrinsic lack of principle and an intrinsic blindness to all value. This means that the sympathy of the spectator, the person who is making the moral judgement, as well as acting as a link in a causal chain, has to be both regulated in some way and made sensitive to utilitarian values. Thus, on the one hand, the spectator is called upon to make certain empirical judgements. On the other hand, in so far as these judgements are part of a proposed explanation of what it is to make a moral judgement they must be practical judgements. But although the judgements which are designed to rectify the shortcomings of the spectator's immediate sympathy may incidentally affect the spectator's feelings they do not necessarily do this; and they therefore cannot be regarded as examples of practical reasoning. Therefore, to whatever else the unsatisfactoriness of the sympathetic theory of moral judgement is to be ultimately attributed, it is not to Hume's debatable concept of practical reason. Even if Hume had developed a more sophisticated concept of practical reason the same impasse would have been encountered.

V

SYMPATHY AND MORAL JUDGEMENT

THE ground on which I have criticized Hume's sympathetic theory of moral judgement is that the element of reasoning which must be injected into the account, first, to provide an antidote to the natural prejudice of sympathy and, secondly, to do justice to Hume's utilitarianism, cannot be considered to be practical reasoning. It is still possible to ask, though, whether by modifying the theory in some way there is any chance of rehabilitation. Or is it the case that the whole conception of sympathy functioning as the medium of moral judgement is misguided? Especially we may ask, would a wider understanding of the concept of sympathy make any difference?

If we draw the distinction between sympathy as a conative force and sympathy as a disseminator of feelings, then there is a strong case for supposing that Hume's understanding is limited almost exclusively to the latter. I tried to show in Chapter II how this limited outlook is reflected in Hume's genesis of sympathy. Remember how awkward Hume found it when he had to explain why when we sympathize with a beggar we should ever feel moved to help him as opposed to avoiding him as something disgusting. For if, as according to Hume, to sympathize with another is merely to have the same feeling as he has, then it is necessary to appeal to something more than the mere fact of sympathy in order to explain why we should want to alleviate misery and distress instead of passing by on the other side. The analogy between the moral feelings and the indirect passions shows that Hume must still be thinking of sympathy in the same terms when in Book Three he comes on to explain the nature of moral judgement.

This distinction between fellow-feeling as merely feeling what another is feeling and fellow-feeling as involving a concern to help the other should not be understood as meaning merely that sometimes we feel like helping the person with whom we sympathize and sometimes we do not. Rather, as I emphasized in Chapter I when I discussed and set up my 'purified' concept of sympathy, an attitude of concern must be seen as central to the notion of practical fellow-feeling or sympathy proper. We can further bring out the difference between mere fellow-feeling and sympathy proper by saying that in the first the attention of the subject is focused on the feeling he is experiencing and need not go beyond this, whilst in the second he is aware of the feeling and at the same time knows that this feeling *really belongs to another person*. That is, in sympathy we concentrate on the feeling as being felt by another individual rather than as something which, as part of our own consciousness, is not necessarily related to any other centre of consciousness. Consequently, in fellow-feeling we remain indifferent to the source of our vicarious feeling, whilst in sympathy we are, on the contrary, actively interested in the other person and his predicament. It seems that for Hume 'sympathy' was in most cases equivalent to 'fellow-feeling': he seems to have been captivated by a picture of sympathy as the communication of feeling. I hope this was clearly brought out by my discussion of his account of the genesis of sympathy and the nature of the illustrations of sympathy he gives.

The question now is whether the sympathetic theory of moral evaluation can be made any more viable through the introduction of this different definition of 'sympathy'. I think that the answer to this must be in the negative. The main reason for thinking this is that Hume's theory demands a *medium* for it to make sense. Sympathy acts as a link in a causal chain. In so far as Hume thought of approval and disapproval as objective variants of the indirect passions of love and hate, he would be bound to give analogous explanations of their origins. Just as sympathy is an indispensable part of the mechanism of love and hatred so it is an indispensable part of the mechanism of approval and disapproval. In so far as it provides us with a sense in which we can understand how feeling can be communicated from one person to another, sympathy fulfils this role. But it is clear that for sympathy to fulfil this role successfully we need only understand it as a *disseminator of feeling*. The introduction of the separate notion of *conative sympathy* is therefore not really helpful to Hume's position. We have seen the trouble the requirement of impartiality caused Hume; but this is not to be avoided by bringing in the notion of conative sympathy. Although there is always a sense in which my sympathetic feelings are necessarily my own feelings, at the same time it makes sense to say that through conative sympathy we are provided with some kind of awareness of another's feelings which is rather different from merely knowing that he is experiencing certain feelings. Such sympathy broadens our horizons, partially releases us from the egocentric predicament and informs us of the needs of others. But to say that sympathy makes us interested in the needs of others is not to say anything about the *status* of these needs; it is not to say anything about *your* needs and their claim to be satisfied in relation to *my* needs and their claim to be satisfied. The fact that I sympathize with someone does not necessarily mean that I am going to treat his needs on a par with my own. It is certainly true that sympathy shows us that others count, but does it show us for *how much* they count? Does my sympathy with another show me that his interests count for as much as or more than my own? If I sympathize with another then I am disposed to help him—this is the conative element—but notice that I am only 'disposed' to help him. If helping him would be against my own interests then I have a reason for not doing so (although this reason is not necessarily an over-riding one). If helping him would be against the law or against someone else's interests (especially if I stood in a special relation to that third person) then these would be further (and perhaps better) reasons for not acting in the man's interests. So although the fact that I sympathize with another is a reason for helping him, it is not an unassailable reason and may on occasions have to be weighed against the requirements of justice and the obligations special relations impose upon us. Furthermore, conative sympathy is just as likely to be conditioned by such contingent circumstances as time, place, mood, interest, and so on, as mere infectious fellow-feeling is. Conative sympathy is just as partial and variable, and therefore just as in need of qualification by reason, as infectious fellow-feeling.

It follows that if Hume's theory of moral judgement is unsatisfactory then it is unsatisfactory no matter in what sense 'sympathy' is understood. This unsatisfactoriness is not the outcome of Hume's particular concept of sympathy any more than it is the outcome of his particular concept of practical reason. The weakness of Hume's account can be traced to his fundamental belief that moral judgement was to be conceived in terms of a special moral sentiment the occurrence of which could be explained in terms of associationist principles. The need for a medium of moral judgement is inextricably bound up with this belief.

The particular connection between sympathy and moral judgement which the *Treatise* envisages is not the only way in which it has been thought that sympathy is relevant to moral judgement. A brief look at the place of sympathy in a contemporary version of the moral sentiment theory will, I hope, confirm the view that the whole enterprise of seeking to explain moral judgement in terms of sympathetic feeling is futile. Despite Adam Smith's more sophisticated account of the relation between the concepts of individuality and society, ultimately his account of moral judgement does not seem any more tenable than Hume's. In *The Theory of Moral Sentiments* (1759) Smith devotes a great deal of space to a discussion of the nature of sympathy. He does not entirely agree with Hume's views here. Although, like Hume, he thinks that to sympathize with another is to come to have the same feelings as this other person has, Smith does not conceive the process by which this happens in Hume's mechanical terms. Whereas Hume held that sympathy consists in the idea of an emotion being converted into the emotion itself through the enlivening association with the impression of self, according to Smith sympathy involves imagining oneself in the other person's situation and thus, in one's imagination, going through all the emotional experiences he would be going through. We change places 'in fancy with the sufferer' (*T.M.S.*, p. 258). Smith's concept is altogether more catholic than Hume's; from his copious illustrations it would seem that he wants to admit pity and compassion, fellow-feeling, infection, and even empathy,[1] all as varieties of sympathy. The result of this is that some of his pronouncements about 'sympathy' are inconsistent with one another. In general, though, he tends to see sympathy as a rather more intellectual concept than Hume does; for instance, our sympathy with another is said to be 'always extremely imperfect' until we know the cause of the other's feelings (*T.M.S.*, p. 261). It is the situation in which the other is placed, as much as his personal response to it, which gives rise to

---

[1] 'The mob, when they are gazing at a dancer on the slack rope, naturally writhe and twist and balance their bodies, as they see him do, and as they feel that they themselves must do it in his situation' (*T.M.S.*, p. 258). The spectator watching the acrobat presents the typical case of 'empathy'. Some degree of identification with the acrobat will cause in the spectator certain motor-impulses which are correlated with those of the acrobat. But understood in this sense, 'empathy' is of no ethical interest.

our sympathy. Perhaps Smith's most serious confusion stems from his failure to clarify whether sympathy involves imagining what one would feel if one were in the other's situation or whether it involves imagining oneself as the other person.[1] Towards the end of *The Theory of Moral Sentiments* there is an emphatic statement of the second view:

> When I condole with you for the loss of your only son, in order to enter into your grief I do not consider what I, a person of such a character and profession, should suffer, if I had a son, and if that son were unfortunately to die: but I consider what I should suffer, if I was really you, and I do not only change circumstances with you, but I change persons and characters. (*T.M.S.*, p. 323.)

Although it may call for a little more imaginative effort than otherwise, the fact that I have no children does not create an obstacle to my sympathizing with someone who has lost a child. On the other hand, the examples in Smith's opening chapter suggest the first view. Thus it is said that through sympathy I may blush with embarrassment at the stupidity of another 'though he himself appears to have no sense of the impropriety of his own behaviour' (*T.M.S.*, p. 261). And of our sympathy with 'the poor wretch . . . altogether insensible of his own misery', Smith comments:

> The anguish which humanity feels . . . at the sight of such an object, cannot be the reflection of any sentiment of the sufferer. The compassion of the spectator must arise altogether from the consideration of what he himself would feel if he were reduced to the same unhappy situation, and, what perhaps is impossible, was at the same time able to regard it with his present reason and judgment. (*T.M.S.*, p. 262.)

Understood in this sense, 'sympathy' does not even seem to entail that the sympathetic agent must experience the same feeling as the other person. The question whether or not I sympathize with a certain person will then depend on how *I* would respond if *I* were placed in his circumstances.

---

[1] Butler, in his sermon 'Upon Compassion', clearly recognizes this distinction. Speaking about Hobbes's suggestion that compassion amounts only to fear for ourselves, Butler says: '. . . if there be anything of this sort common to mankind, distinct from the reflection of reason, it would be a most remarkable instance of what was farthest from his thoughts, namely, of a mutual sympathy between each particular of the species, a fellow-feeling common to mankind. It would not indeed be an example of our substituting others for ourselves, but it would be an example of substituting ourselves for others.' (*Fifteen Sermons*, p. 409n.)

It is possible to see the connection between this latter view of sympathy and the theory of moral judgement which Smith puts forward. A remark such as 'I don't sympathize with him at all—he always makes a fuss about nothing' suggests not only that the speaker would not have reacted himself in the way the other person had done but also an attitude of scornful impatience and *disapproval* on the speaker's part. If a magistrate says to a defendant 'I cannot sympathize with anyone who wants to take drugs' then not only is he saying that he cannot really imagine why anyone from his own free will should want to indulge in drug-taking but also (and in this context most importantly) that he *disapproves* of the desire and its satisfaction. In so far as his remark anticipates a stern sentence the magistrate is using 'sympathize' to express a value judgement; in this sense, 'sympathizing' with someone is close in meaning to 'going along' with someone. Now Smith has fastened on this use of 'sympathy' and has, as we shall see, developed it as the basis of his moral theory. This is apparent before he has begun to expound this theory:

In every passion of which the mind of man is susceptible, the emotions of the by-stander always correspond to what, by bringing the case home to himself, he imagines *should be* the sentiments of the sufferer.[1] (*T.M.S.*, p. 259.)

Smith denies that there is such a thing as a moral faculty or sense. He thinks that moral approval and disapproval are based on special feelings in much the same way as Hume does. Although there is agreement between Hume and Smith that these feelings are connected with the sympathetic feelings of the person who makes the moral judgement, this agreement does not extend to the identity of the object of this sympathy or to other important details. On Smith's account, our approval and disapproval are closely connected with our sympathy with the *agent's motives and sentiments*. When I realize that I sympathize with someone else's feelings then I must necessarily approve of them and correspondingly when I realize that I cannot sympathize with them I must disapprove of them.

When the original passions of the person principally concerned are in perfect concord with the sympathetic emotions of the spectator,

----

[1] My italics.

they necessarily appear to this last just and proper, and suitable to their objects; and, on the contrary, when, upon bringing the case home to himself, he finds that they do not coincide with what he feels, they necessarily appear to him unjust and improper, and unsuitable to the causes which excite them. To approve of the passions of another, therefore, as suitable to their objects, is the same thing as to observe that we entirely sympathize with them; and not to approve of them as such, is the same thing as to observe that we do not entirely sympathize with them. (*T.M.S.*, pp. 267–8.)

I do not sympathize because I approve—rather I approve because I sympathize. The sentiment of approbation is a compound feeling, analysable not only into this sympathy with the motives and feelings of the agent but also into: (a) sympathy with the gratitude of the beneficiaries of the agent's conduct; (b) satisfaction on observing that the agent's conduct 'has been agreeable to the general rules by which these two sympathies generally act'; and (c) satisfaction on the observation that the agent's conduct exemplifies a kind of conduct which fits into a scheme of things conducive to the well-being of the individual and/or his society— a feeling comparable to that which the contemplation of a well-contrived machine arouses in us. (See *T.M.S.*, pp. 334–5.) Whenever I esteem another's behaviour as virtuous the moral feeling on which this evaluation depends is in every instance analysable into these four distinct feelings. A corresponding analysis can be given for the feeling of disapprobation. Thus although Smith's moral feelings differ from Hume's in that they are not discrete and unanalysable, they are similar in that they are not to be regarded merely as a species of sympathetic feeling themselves. Although Smith refuses to base approbation and disapprobation directly on utility (*T.M.S.*, p. 273), it is clear from the above analysis that in so far as sympathy with the beneficiaries of the agent's act together with satisfaction on the observation of the way in which the agent's conduct conduces to the well-being of the individual and/or society form a necessary part of the moral feelings, Smith recognizes that some element of utility is essential to evaluation. He adds that even if on an occasion we find that we cannot sympathize with the other person, we may still be able to approve of his conduct in so far as we realize that in normal circumstances we should sympathize with his feelings and motives.

As for the moral judgements we make upon ourselves, Smith explains these by reference to his famous 'well-informed and impartial spectator'. In order to evaluate our own conduct and attitudes we have to consider how far such a spectator could sympathize with our own motives and feelings.

We endeavour to examine our own conduct as we imagine any other fair and impartial spectator would examine it. If, upon placing ourselves in his situation, we thoroughly enter into all the passions and motives which influenced it, we approve of it, by sympathy with the approbation of this supposed equitable judge. If otherwise, we enter into his disapprobation, and condemn it. (*T.M.S.*, p. 298.)

Notice here that sympathy enters into this explanation at two entirely separate stages: (a) the imaginary impartial spectator's sympathy with the agent's motives and feelings; and (b) the agent's sympathy with the impartial spectator's verdict on himself, the agent. Another point worth noting in this connection is that Smith does *not* say that in *all* our moral judgements we consider what an impartial spectator would feel, that is, including those judgements we make about others, but that we do this only in those judgements we make about ourselves.

The net outcome is that each member of the community, being by way of sympathy so sharply sensitive to the feelings of his fellows, will endeavour all the while to harmonize his own feelings, or at least the expression of these feelings, with those of his neighbours. We do not expect a stranger to take a great interest in our personal affairs since we realize that he is not in a position to enter very fully into our feelings. Consequently, we temper the expression of our feelings in his presence and expect him to do likewise. What passes for appropriate behaviour, appropriate expression of feelings, in one context (that is, among individuals each standing to the others in some mutually recognized or recognizable relation) will not be acceptable, and may well be intolerable, in a different context. This social harmony is achieved through each member of the community

lowering his passion to that pitch in which the spectators are capable of going along with him. He must flatten . . . the sharpness of its natural tone, in order to reduce it to harmony and concord with the emotions of those who are about him. What they feel, will indeed always be, in some respects, different from what he feels, and compassion can never be exactly the same with original sorrow. . . . Though they will never be unisons, they may be concords, and this is all that is wanted or required. (*T.M.S.*, pp. 275–6.)

To bring Smith's point to life it is worth quoting an extract from Albert Camus's *The Plague*. He is describing the behaviour of the city's inhabitants two months after the plague has set in:

> . . . in this extremity of solitude none could count on any help from his neighbour; each had to bear the load of his troubles alone. If, by some chance, one of us tried to unburden himself or to say something about his feelings, the reply he got, whatever it might be, usually wounded him. And then it dawned on him that he and the man with him weren't talking about the same thing. For while he himself spoke from the depths of long days of brooding upon his personal distress, and the image he had tried to impart had been slowly shaped and proved in the fires of passion and regret, this meant nothing to the man to whom he was speaking, and who pictured a conventional emotion, a grief that is traded on the market-place, mass-produced. Whether friendly or hostile, the reply always missed fire, and the attempt to communicate had to be given up. This was true of those at least for whom silence was unbearable, and since the others could not find the truly expressive word, they resigned themselves to using the current coin of language, the commonplaces of plain narrative, of anecdote, and their daily paper. So, in these cases, too, even the sincerest grief had to make do with the set phrases of ordinary conversation. Only on these terms could the prisoners of the plague ensure the sympathy of their door-porter and the interest of their hearers. (*The Plague*, p. 64.)

But it is equally as true of the normal state of affairs—as well as of this extraordinary state of affairs—that each of us has to make sure that the feelings he makes public are fit for trading in the market-place. According to Smith, this tempering of emotion in response to the sympathy of our fellows gives rise to two sets of virtues. On the one hand, the effort of the spectator to enter into the feelings of the agent gives rise to the 'soft, the gentle, the amiable virtues, the virtues of candid condescension and indulgent humanity'; and the other, the effort of the agent to bring down the intensity of his feelings to a level with which the spectator can be expected to go along gives rise to 'the great, the awful and the respectable, the virtues of self-denial, of self-government, of that command of the passions'. (See *T.M.S.*, pp. 277–8.)

What is particularly interesting about Adam Smith's account of the relation between sympathy and moral approval is that it seems to display an awareness of the relation of man to society which is rather unexpected in view of the streak of excessive individualism with which he is often credited. It is possible to detect in much of Smith's thought on the topic a certain shift of emphasis from a simple consideration of the individual in isolation to a consideration of him in the context of the society in which he lives—a shift of interest which opens up the way for what it might not be an exaggeration to describe as a sociological understanding of the nature of moral phenomena. Of the two aspects of Smith's thinking I have found this one the more profitable and stimulating to explore.

In so far as he tries to see moral phenomena against a background of a society all the parts of which influence and respond to each other, Smith seems to want to suggest that sympathy operates as the major regulating force within this society—in much the same way as a governor functions so as to maintain a constant speed in a piece of machinery. Now the trouble is that whilst Smith has this valuable, but at the same time limited, insight into the nature of the connection between a man's moral beliefs and his social context, it seems to lead him to imply some quite unacceptable things about the meaning of moral language. That I sympathize with a person, it is justifiably objected, does not imply that I necessarily approve of that person's character or conduct. It is true that a particular use of 'sympathy' (exemplified when I say that I 'withhold' my sympathy from someone) does imply a value judgement; but in such a case the reason I do not sympathize is that I do not (for reasons quite unconnected with sympathy) approve in the first place. The account of the judgements we make about others might have been more plausible had Smith made use of the device of the impartial and well-informed spectator; but even to have done this would have eventually involved his account in the same sort of difficulties concerning practical reason as I discussed in connection with Hume. It is hard to deny that he identifies 'the moral' with what is acceptable or respectable in the community. It is impossible for the individual member of society to break out of Smith's circle of reciprocal sympathy in order to demand whether the standards according to which he lives his life are worthwhile standards or even whether they are the only standards possible. He cannot sensibly question the conventional morality of the society in which he happens to find himself. In Smith's account it does not make sense to say anything like: 'I have always believed that X is the right thing to do and everyone else thinks so too, but I'm not so sure about it now.' For having drawn attention to the coincidence of one's own approbation with that of the rest of society, there remain no more considerations which can be brought to bear on the question whether or not X is the right thing to do. There is no question of advancing reasons to back up one's moral attitudes and beliefs. It is true that Smith does allow that there are 'general rules' by which we 'correct' any wayward sympathetic feelings (*T.M.S.*, p. 304); but on close examination these rules turn out to be mere generalizations of what in the past we have approved and disapproved of and they are therefore circular. There are two particularly serious defects in Smith's theory. The first is that he cannot leave room for the possibility of discussion and genuine disagreement in moral discourse. Abortion, drug-taking, draft-dodging : these are all issues over which there is considerable discussion and many shades of opinion. But if moral judgement were merely a matter of consulting one's sympathetic feelings then these problems would be quickly disposed of without the need for advancing any reasons or arguments. The other principal defect in Smith's account is that it cannot explain how moral attitudes can change within a given society; how, for instance, a society can grow more puritanical or humanitarian or permissive. For Smith morality is something given and static. In short, Smith may be able to suggest to us something of value about how sympathy functions so as to perpetuate and stabilize particular attitudes and beliefs within a society and how in doing this it helps to preserve the identity of that society; but he cannot adequately explain why a society conforms to the standards it does and not to others, how the individual member of society comes to hold the attitudes he does or how it is possible for these standards and attitudes to be questioned and to change.

This regulative function of sympathy in society is important and something more should be said about it. It is clearly recognized by Sidgwick in *The Methods of Ethics*. There he distinguishes two ways in which sympathy acts as a regulative force :

. . . the moral impulses of each individual commonly draw a large part of their effective force from the sympathy of other human beings. I do not merely mean that the pleasures and pains which each derives sympathetically from the moral likings and aversions of others are important as motives to felicific conduct no less than as elements of the individual's happiness : I mean further that the direct sympathetic echo in each man of the judgements and sentiments of others concerning conduct sustains his own similar judgements and sentiments. Through this twofold operation of sympathy it becomes practically much easier for most men to conform to a moral rule established in the society to which they belong than to one made by themselves. And any act by which a man weakens the effect on himself of this general moral sympathy tends *pro tanto* to make the performance of duty more difficult for him. (*The Methods of Ethics*, pp. 482–3.)

Thus in the first way sympathy can be seen as functioning directly as a motive to encourage some kinds of conduct and discourage others. In so far as our conduct elicits certain emotional responses in others and in so far as we, as agents, sympathize with these responses we shall tend to repeat that conduct which leads to pleasant sympathetic feelings and avoid that which leads to unpleasant sympathetic feelings. Thus it is that other people's blame and praise influence our behaviour; as Hume says, 'the uneasiness of being contemn'd depends on sympathy' (*T.H.N.*, p. 322). In its second regulative capacity, sympathy with the judgements and attitudes of others 'sustains' our own judgements and attitudes when these happen to coincide with one another. The realization —through the sympathetic experience—of the coincidence of one's own feelings with the feelings of others tends to confirm and lend authority to those feelings. In either of these two capacities 'sympathy' need only be thought of as infectious fellow-feeling, although, of course, both passive fellow-feeling and conative fellow-feeling (sympathy) will exert the same influence. The over-all effect of this double operation of sympathy is to stabilize and standardize certain attitudes and certain kinds of conduct to the exclusion of certain others. It explains the difficulty experienced in deliberately flying in the face of social opinion and expectation. Notice that, contrary to what Smith maintains about the connection between sympathy and approval, it is quite possible for me to sympathize with another's feeling of approval towards X whilst quite sincerely disapproving of X myself. Finally, in so far as sympathy has a regulative influence on attitudes, beliefs, and values within a society in the two ways described, it is quite clear that these attitudes, beliefs, and values must already be in existence and cannot in any sense be generated by or derived from sympathy.

Before leaving Smith's moral theory I think it is worth examining in a little more detail his account of the moral judgements we make upon our own conduct and attitudes. According to this account, when I say that I feel remorse or that my conscience pricks me I imply that I have sympathized with the disapproval which I judge an impartial and well-informed spectator would feel on the contemplation of my own conduct or feelings. Now I think this account raises at least two important questions. The first is whether or not when we make self-judgements of this kind we are necessarily sympathizing with a spectator, real or imaginary. Is there a prima facie reason for supposing that this is the only way in which we can come to ascribe moral worth to our own conduct or feelings? The unavoidable implication of Smith's view seems to be that if I am thought to be guilty then I am guilty; or more accurately, when I realize that I am thought to be guilty then I feel guilty and this is equivalent to being guilty. But this is an absurd position to have to maintain. It is true that other people's estimates of ourselves affect us—sometimes very strongly—and that this may be explained in terms of fellow-feeling, both cognitive and non-cognitive. But on those occasions when our behaviour is motivated by such factors, when we are willing to bow before social opinion, it is extremely doubtful whether we recognize the specifically *moral* authority of social opinion; rather, our reason for such conformity is not respect for any such authority but expediency and a desire for social harmony. To put it another way: the fact that others can persuade or coerce me into believing that X is right or wrong is not what makes X right or wrong. Whether he likes it or not, sympathy as communication of feeling acts on each and every member of society, profoundly influencing his behaviour. This fact is recognized and deliberately and subtly exploited by teachers, politicians, advertisers, psychiatrists, and others interested in manipulating thought and behaviour. But from a moral point of view it does not seem to matter whether we hold the beliefs and try to realize the values we do because we have been threatened or bribed or because our capacity for fellow-feeling has been exploited or because this capacity has manifested itself in its usual insidious fashion. Although these all constitute possible explanations why we hold certain beliefs and pursue certain ends, they do not amount to moral justifications of these beliefs and ends. Furthermore, it is also true that another's adverse opinion of oneself may, once we have recovered from our initial resentment and scepticism, prompt self-scrutiny; but this activity must be distinguished from those of self-condemnation and self-approval. Finally, it is also true that when deciding what to do in a complicated situation we shall look at it from various points of view, those of others as well as our own; and that these preliminary reflections call for a sympathetic attitude towards others. But in this sense we have to understand 'sympathy', not just as the capacity for passive infection, but at least as the capacity to enter freely into the feelings of others, and possibly to be concerned for these others as well. Despite all this, it does not follow that we are unable to evaluate our own conduct and feelings immediately and without having recourse to the device of sympathizing with some imaginary spectator.

But if for Smith the moral is equivalent to the respectable and the impartial and well-informed spectator no more than the embodiment of social opinion, we should be unwise to jump to the conclusion that Hume's version of the sympathetic theory shares the same unpalatable implication. Smith's impartial spectator and 'general rules' are paralleled in Hume's version by the notion of sympathizing from a general point of view (in so far as we interpret this as including the making of utility judgements). Hume maintains that we must take up this standpoint whether we are judging our own or someone else's case. On the surface Hume's position does not look much different from Smith's; but if we think back to what was said in Chapter III it should be clear that Hume distinguishes, though not very obviously, between the general point of view and the majority point of view. The two are not coincident. On Hume's theory, the fact that no-one has ever thought X to be good does not preclude the possibility of its being good. In theory, at least, Hume does not identify the moral with the respectable—despite what critics from T. H. Green[1] to Dorothea Krook[2] say. Confusion has possibly arisen out of Hume's restricted application of the terms 'approval' and 'disapproval'. (See Chapter III.) Although his account allows the possibility that a minority or even no-one at all should think that what is good is good, in practice Hume scarcely entertains the suggestion. It is this same complacency that allows him both to subscribe to the myth that public and private interests coincide and to believe in a 'uniformity in the *general* sentiments of mankind' (*Treatise*, p. 547).

The second issue which Smith's account of self-judgement raises is the relevance that the whole notion of impartiality has for morality. Is the characteristic moral situation one in which recourse to an impartial spectator or judge is appropriate? Is the implicit legal model an adequate model? Is the impartial point

---

[1] *Works*, p. 371.   [2] *Three Traditions of Moral Thought*, pp. 173 f.

of view *the* moral point of view? I shall be discussing these very
important questions in Chapter VII and for the moment I shall
confine myself to merely drawing attention to their existence.

To summarize this present chapter. Although both Hume and
Smith agree that moral judgement is an exercise of sentiment
rather than of reason and that this moral sentiment is to be
explained in terms of the sympathetic feelings of the person who
makes the moral judgement, they do not agree as to the nature
of the connection between this sympathy and the moral sentiment
or as to what constitutes the appropriate object of the sympathy.
For Hume the spectator's sympathy is causally connected with the
moral sentiment; the latter is an unanalysable feeling quite distinct from the sympathy by which it is aroused. By contrast,
Smith's moral sentiment is analysable into four constituent
feelings of, as the case may be, satisfaction or uneasiness; and of
these, two are unmediated feelings of sympathy, namely, sympathy with the motives and feelings of the agent himself and
sympathy with the gratitude or resentment felt by those directly
affected by the agent's conduct. But, as we have seen, for Hume
the object of the mediating sympathy is the satisfaction or uneasiness of the agent himself and/or that of his associates. Another
major difference is that for Hume approval is tied to sympathetic
pleasure, and disapproval to sympathetic pain; whilst for Smith,
in the case of the sympathy with the agent's motives and feelings,
it is the presence of sympathy as such which is connected with
approval and the absence of sympathy as such which is connected
with disapproval. According to Smith, to say that you sympathize
with a criminal is to suggest that you endorse his character and
activities. As they stand, both accounts suffer from the fact that
sympathy is both capricious and blind to value. In order to overcome the first shortcoming Hume introduces the idea of sympathizing from an objective point of view; and although he does
not explicitly say as much, in so far as the value-blindness of sympathy is to be rectified this must mean the introduction of some
kind of utility judgement into Hume's account. But, as I have
tried in the previous chapter to show, these modifications only
lead to a dead end. On the other hand, except in the case of self-
evaluation, Smith refuses to counter these limitations of sympathy
by any external appeals, either to objectivity or to considerations
of utility. As a consequence, his theory of moral sentiment suffers
from an oppressive circularity.

It looks therefore that if we want to explain moral judgement in terms of sympathy we end up with one of two alternatives, each in its own way unsatisfactory: either Hume's inconsistency or Smith's circularity. Neither Hume nor Smith seem to have distinguished sufficiently clearly between the question 'What is it to make a moral judgement?' and the question 'How are moral beliefs and attitudes disseminated and standardized?' The yearning to be accepted and well-thought-of by our fellows, together with the associated tendencies to accept or at least pay lip-service to the prevalent morality of the group with which we most strongly identify ourselves or to which we most strongly aspire and to reject those groups and individuals whose ideas and behaviour threaten and undermine this moral code or way of life, are all to be at least partially elucidated in terms of sympathy, whether infectious, passive, or conative fellow-feeling. But to allow that sympathy exerts a constant and powerful psychological force on each member of society, to allow that it is in this sense a socializing force of vital importance, is quite different from saying that for someone to make a moral judgement necessarily involves being sympathetically affected by the feelings of certain other people. In the remaining chapters I want to turn attention from the idea of sympathy as infection and passive fellow-feeling to what seems to be, ethically at any rate, the more fruitful idea of sympathy as an active concern for another.

VI

SYMPATHY AND VALUE

ALTHOUGH the enterprise of using sympathy to explain the nature of moral judgement has proved unsatisfactory, it would be wrong to infer from this failure on the part of both Hume and Smith that sympathy is anything but an extremely important concept for morality. In this and the following chapter I wish to examine other ways in which sympathy may be thought to be relevant to morality. Not surprisingly, in view of his limited concept of sympathy, Hume showed little interest in the possibility of sympathetic feeling as a motive for action; and in the present chapter I intend to make good this omission by discussing what value could be attached to sympathy seen in this light. If the Kantian belief in the autonomy of reason in ethics can be attacked then one of the ways of doing this is to draw attention to conative sympathy. A consideration of the value of sympathy as a motive will inevitably mean broaching the whole problem of the role of the emotions in morality and in particular the extent to which the sort of position Kant puts forward (which has proved very influential) is open to criticism. In short, are we to agree with Kant that reference to a man's emotions is utterly irrelevant to an assessment of his character and conduct?

In moral evaluation I think it is true to say that we recognize a basic distinction between motives and actions. The considerations which are brought to bear on the question of the morality or immorality of a particular motive are different from the considerations which are brought to bear on the rightness or wrongness of a particular action. A morally valuable motive may issue in a wrong action; and an immoral or neutral motive may issue in a right action. Thus if one were to say that sympathy as a motive is always good this does not commit one to saying anything about the rightness or wrongness of actions motivated by sympathy. This is an important distinction for this chapter. The question of the value of sympathy splits itself into the question of the value of sympathy as a motive and the question of the value of the sympathetic action. In connection with the first, I want to discuss in particular the suggestion that the sympathetic motive is unconditionally valuable; and in connection with the second, that sympathetic action is *prima facie* right and desirable action. After which I shall say something about the possibility of sympathy as an alternative to conscientiousness.

Now there are two principal objections to the suggestion that sympathy as a motive, as a conative attitude towards another, possesses unconditional moral value. The first states that it cannot be morally valuable to sympathize with unworthy emotions such as spite, malice, and envy; and that therefore not all sympathy is valuable. In answering this objection, to begin with I think we can refer once again to the distinction between sympathizing with emotions and sympathizing with individuals. Compare the following statements: (a) 'There were people all round me, fighting and throwing things at the police—and I just got carried away.' (b) 'I could see that she was terribly upset. I knew just how she was feeling and so naturally I wanted to do everything I could to help.' The first speaker was obviously infected by the feelings of the crowd of which he was a member; equally clearly, the second speaker felt genuinely sympathetic towards the other person. The point I wish to make is that infectious sympathy, being involuntary and excluding the possibility of concern for another, must be sharply distinguished from conative sympathy. Therefore, instances of infection by unworthy feelings do not count against the claim that sympathy proper is a motive possessing unconditional value.

But, even having disposed of the infectious situations, it could still be argued that there remains a hard core of instances of genuine conative sympathy with people whose feelings are morally reprehensible. Let us consider some examples. Suppose that I have privileged access to a drug cupboard; and also that I have a friend who is addicted to heroin; and further, that because his normal means of supply has been cut off he is suffering bad withdrawal symptoms. Now in such a situation, if, out of sympathy with the addict, I decide to procure him the drugs he needs, could we not then say that I was sympathizing with someone whose feelings were morally undesirable and that consequently my sympathy itself was undesirable? In answer to this, it can be pointed out, first of all, that a large proportion of one's moral doubts about this particular case stem from the illegality of the

sympathetic *action*, that is, the procuring of the heroin, and
secondly, that to sympathize with someone whose way of life
may be thought morally undesirable and even degenerate does
not mean that this sympathetic attitude is in the least contaminated
or made unworthy itself. The point is that to sympathize with
a person is not to endorse that person's character or way of life.
To sympathize with someone who is envious or spiteful or
malicious does not mean that one is envious or spiteful or malicious oneself. Suppose that Smith is envious of Jones because
Jones has a better job than Smith and that Smith's wife, realizing
this, takes the next opportunity to do Jones a bad turn. The
question is whether Smith's wife could be said to sympathize
with Smith, whether her motive for harming Jones could be
sympathy for Smith. By way of answering this question I want to
consider the distinction between helping a person and helping
a person to do something, or, in other words, assisting him.
According to this distinction, by helping someone to do something I may not be helping *him* and may even be positively harming *him*. Such would be the case if I lent my car to someone the
worse for drink so that he could get home. Now conative sympathy entails a disposition to help the other person, but not to
help him to do something. In some cases the best way of helping
someone is by omitting to offer him our assistance. Thus if
Smith's wife sincerely thought that by hurting Jones she was
helping her husband—as opposed to helping him to do or get
something—we should have to say that her motive was one of
sympathy, even if her action was both misguided and wrong. But
this does not mean that her sympathy for her husband was in itself
undesirable. In fact, the most appropriate way of helping someone who is particularly subject to such feelings as spite and envy
would probably be to help him overcome them. In so far as we
sympathize with him we should have to enter into these feelings
of spite and envy; but this does not mean that we should be
envious or spiteful ourselves or that in helping him out of sympathy we should encourage him to foster such feelings or direct
his attention to fresh objects for them. If we did so then we should
be harming not helping him. Of course, I do not want to suggest
that it is a simple matter to show someone else how to alter his
disposition towards the rest of the world. In such cases the help
one can envisage would be of a very indirect kind. In Smith's
situation it is likely that he is not only envious of Jones's superior

job but also basically unhappy about the whole state of affairs. Our concern for him could then take the shape of trying to alleviate this basic unhappiness, possibly by commiserating with him and giving him the opportunity to ventilate his grievances.

Thus sympathy with those whose feelings, whole character, or way of life may be thought to be morally undesirable does not mean that this sympathy itself is morally suspect. To imagine that it does have this effect stems from one or other of three mistakes : (a) confusing sympathy with infection; (b) failing to distinguish the sympathetic motive from the sympathetic action; and (c) thinking that sympathizing entails assisting rather than helping the other person. Above all, we sympathize with people—not with feelings. So long as we bear these points in mind, we can see that there can be no objection to saying that we can sympathize with the landlord who exploits the widow in just the same way as we can sympathize with the widow herself and further that the value of the sympathy is the same in each case.

The second objection to the suggestion that the motive of sympathy is unconditionally good is based on the supposition that sympathy is an instinctive response. We cannot choose to be sympathetic towards another person and therefore sympathy must be morally neutral. This criticism is a very serious one and cannot possibly be given a satisfactory answer without raising the whole issue of the place of emotion in morality. But before embarking on this topic, I wish to distinguish the present thesis for which I am arguing from one with which it may be confused, namely, that sympathy is the only moral motive. Such a thesis would identify moral value with the motive of sympathy : to act sympathetically would be to act morally and to act without sympathy would be to act neutrally or immorally. Such a position is similar, though somewhat simplified, to that which Schopenhauer wants to maintain in *On the Basis of Morality* (pp. 120–98). But such a claim does not really stand up; mainly because it implies a drastic revaluation of the motives of conscientiousness. We are flattered if someone describes us as 'sympathetic' and disappointed if as 'unsympathetic'. It is fair to say that the view that sympathetic feeling is an admirable motive from which to act is a view with which few people would ordinarily want to quarrel. Moreover, to this we can add the interesting fact that most people would prefer to receive the help of someone who helped them because he sympathized with them rather than the help of someone who helped them because he thought it was his duty to do so. But although these observations suggest that sympathy possesses more value than some moral philosophers in the past have been willing to accord it and also perhaps that sympathy possesses a certain warmth that is lacking in conscientiousness, they are not reasonable grounds for supposing that sympathy is the sole moral motive. I cannot see what other evidence could be produced in favour of the claim that to act out of sympathy is to act morally and to act without sympathy is at best to act neutrally, at worst immorally.

It should be clear enough that the thesis that the motive of sympathy is unconditionally good leaves room for the possibility that acts performed out of conscientiousness also possess moral value. Nevertheless, in order to sustain this thesis an answer, or rather several answers, have to be found to the Kantian objections to the emotions as possible motives for morally valuable actions. The problem is, therefore, to show that emotionally motivated conduct in general, and sympathetically motivated conduct in particular, may possess moral worth. As I have previously said, this question must be separated from that of the assessment of the rightness or wrongness of the sympathetic action. What I want to discuss then is whether we can say of a sympathetic act that it is morally worthwhile or whether we must agree with Kant that the fact that an act is motivated by sympathy is, at best, of no relevance to the question of its moral value. If we are asked to justify, as opposed to explain, our behaviour, is it appropriate to appeal to our emotions? Or must our answer, if it is to bear any moral weight, be in terms of a recognition that whatever we had done was for the sake of duty? Is it possible to argue that we *ought* to be sympathetic towards others? Or that we can *blame* someone for not being sympathetic? On the one hand, if we are to do justice to the common belief about the moral status of sympathy then it seems that provision has to be made for the view that sympathy is a virtue; and on the other, we are challenged by the uncompromising and apparently strong argument that Kant advances against admitting any moral value to emotionally motivated conduct. Let us consider what Kant has said.

Kant's attitude towards the emotions is focused in the well-known passage where he contrasts the man who acts out of respect for his duty with the man who acts out of sympathetic feeling. Although externally their actions may be identical, only the first man's will possess true moral worth. Although the presence of a natural 'inclination' such as sympathy does not detract from the moral value of the act, it in no way contributes to it. That the motive is respect for the moral law is a necessary and sufficient condition of an action's having moral worth. It is only in so far as an action is performed *for the sake of duty* that it possesses moral value. It is worth quoting the passage in question at length:

To help others where one can is a duty, and besides this there are many spirits of so sympathetic a temper that, without any further motive of vanity or self-interest, they find an inner pleasure in spreading happiness around them and can take delight in the contentment of others as their own work. Yet I maintain that in such a case an action of this kind, however right and however amiable it may be, has still no genuinely moral worth. It stands on the same footing as other inclinations—for example, the inclination for honour, which if fortunate enough to hit on something beneficial and right and consequently honourable, deserves praise and encouragement, but not esteem; for its maxim lacks moral content, namely, the performance of such actions, not from inclination, but *from duty*. Suppose then that the mind of this friend of man were overclouded by sorrows of his own which extinguished all sympathy with the fate of others, but that he still had power to help those in distress, though no longer stirred by the need of others because sufficiently occupied with his own; and suppose that, when no longer moved by any inclination, he tears himself out of this deadly insensibility and does the action without any inclination for the sake of duty alone; then for the first time his action has its genuine moral worth. Still further: if nature had implanted little sympathy in this or that man's heart; if (being in other respects an honest fellow) he were cold in temperament and indifferent to the sufferings of others —perhaps because, being endowed with the special gift of patience and robust endurance in his own sufferings, he assumed the like in others or even demanded it; if such a man (who would in truth not be the worst product of nature) were not exactly fashioned by her to be a philanthropist, would he still not find in himself a source from which he might draw a worth far higher than any that a good-natured temperament can have? Assuredly he would. It is precisely in this that the worth of character begins to show—a moral worth and beyond all comparison the highest—namely, that he does good, not from inclination, but from duty. (*G.M.M.*, p. 66.)

Kant's objection is, therefore, not against sympathy in particular but rather against the emotions as a whole. In so far as sympathy is a product of the passionate side of our nature it counts as an 'inclination'; and to Kant all 'inclinations' are 'on the same foot-ing'. In other passages the emotions are described as being 'pathological' in nature. This view of the passions is the outcome of Kant's belief that morality must be necessarily binding. We are rational creatures; and therefore what is moral is what is binding upon a rational creature. A principle of conduct is right only if it could be accepted by any rational creature whatsoever, irrespective of any contingent attributes it may posesss. To allow oneself to be motivated only by principles of right conduct is to act with a Good Will. To possess a Good Will is therefore to act rationally. It follows that we cannot deliberately choose to act wickedly; and that therefore when we do act wickedly we must be acting irrationally, impulsively, or on inclination. Kant's position is further complicated by his tendency to think that our emotions are delusory and merely an aspect in which the rational being appears to itself. (The difficulty in understanding how we could act wrongly if it were the case that our emotions were delusory is explained away by an appeal to the rather obscure distinction between the noumenal self and the phenomenal self.)

Since I do not wish to be accused of distorting Kant's views it would be as well to point out at once that I do not intend to dis-cuss Kant's moral theory as such. I mention his views in particular because I take them to be representative of the most persistent of the arguments against admitting moral worth to the passionate side of human nature. In his Inaugural Lecture at Bedford College, published as *Morality and the Emotions* (1965), Professor Bernard Williams suggested that there are at least three specific objections made by Kant against the view that emotionally motivated behaviour may possess moral value.[1] In order to avoid quibbling whether or not Kant did make these objections, perhaps it would be better to think of them as 'Kantian' rather than 'Kant's'. (a) Our emotions are capricious. Their strength and constancy depend on our interests, our relations to the other people involved, our particular mood or frame of mind, and many other con-tingencies, none of which are morally relevant factors. (b) Our emotions are not subject to deliberation and choice. They are to be thought of as 'happening to us'. To experience an emotion is to be a *passive* subject. It follows that we cannot be held re-sponsible for our emotions in the same way as we are for our

---

[1] My approach to this question has been influenced by Professor Williams's very interesting paper.

thoughts, attitudes, and beliefs. (c) Individuals do not all possess
the same emotional make-up. Nature may have implanted more
sympathy in this man's heart than that man's. This being so, if
emotionally motivated action possessed moral worth, then when
we came to judge a person's moral character it would be reasonable
to make allowances in view of his natural emotional capacities.
But this is not the case. Morality is no handicap affair. Men are
to be judged as equally capable of leading the good life, of
possessing Good Wills. If there are any excuses and exceptions
then these are not justified by reference to individuals' differing
emotional capacities. By contrast, all men are equally capable of
exerting their rationality. It is interesting to compare these objections with what Hume says about the traditional derogation of
the passions as possible motives for moral conduct:

> . . . nor is there an ampler field . . . than this suppos'd pre-eminence
> of reason above passion. The eternity, invariableness, and divine
> origin of the former have been display'd to the best advantage: The
> blindness, unconstancy and deceitfulness of the latter have been as
> strongly insisted on. (*Treatise*, p. 413.)

Objection (a)—that our emotions are capricious—is very
plausible. To be considered a moral agent is, among other things,
to be considered as capable of acting with some degree of consistency. If on an occasion I say that X is good then I am committing myself to saying the same thing in the same circumstances
in the future. If I consider there are good reasons for acting in the
way I do in a particular situation then I commit myself to the
view that there exist the same good reasons (for myself at least,
if not for others) for acting in the same way in similar situations
in the future. If we are to judge and act with any degree of consistency then we have to have regard for such things as reasons,
principles and policies; we must know what makes the difference
between good and bad reasons, principles, and policies. In terms
of Kant's account, the recognition that it is our duty to perform
a particular act is the supreme and unassailable reason for doing
it. The question arises whether or not emotionally motivated
conduct can exhibit this characteristic consistency. Briefly, the
answer depends upon one's concept of emotion. There is no
doubt that there is a good sense in which the emotions and the
conduct they inspire are capricious. To be generously disposed
towards someone one day merely because I happen to be in high

spirits is not morally commendable if the next day I don't care a damn about him. If in the excitement of winning the pools I start flinging my money about there is nothing morally admirable about this. Similarly, there is nothing distinctively moral about the solicitude and attention a lover shows for his beloved. These kinds of emotionally based behaviour do not commit the agent to similar behaviour in the future. We must admit then that in so far as it is correct to say that some emotionally motivated conduct cannot be backed by justifying reasons it cannot provide us with any grounds for expecting, or requiring, its repetition in the future when circumstances are appropriate; and that in so far as this is so it cannot possess moral worth. But having said this much, we can go on to point out that an uncompromising refusal to admit moral worth to emotionally motivated conduct as a whole is the outcome of, or depends on, a rather crude model of the emotions. This Kantian picture of the emotions appears to be of the kind which lies behind such ideas as the 'spontaneous overflowing of powerful feelings' and the emotions 'running away with us'. Such a picture lends credence to the view that we can only act in one of two ways: either rationally or on temporary impulses. Against this view, though, it can be pointed out that emotions themselves may be rational or irrational, justified or unjustified. Panic at the sight of a mouse may be irrational and unjustified, but not so on being confronted by a madman with an axe. The emotions which we feel in a particular situation are determined by our analysis of that situation in combination with our pre-existing beliefs about the nature of the constituents into which we analyse the situation. These beliefs may be unjustified; but in so far as they are to count as beliefs at all they must have some kind of logic, good or bad, behind them and they must be fairly consistently applied to the appropriate situations by the person who holds them. If this is correct then beliefs, and thus the emotions which may be based upon them, cannot be capricious. Dismay at spilling the salt or delight at crossing paths with a black cat may be irrational feelings; but if the person holds the relevant beliefs about the significance of such occurrences and consistently applies them then these emotions and any behaviour connected with them cannot be considered to be capricious. Therefore, although we have to admit that some emotionally motivated behaviour is capricious, in so far as emotions are susceptible to beliefs and capable of consistent and systematic repetition it cannot be the case that *all* emotionally motivated conduct is necessarily capricious.

Objection (b) was that our emotions 'happen to us'; that they come and go without being subject to any control by the agent. Clearly, this objection is closely bound up with the first in that it, too, has been influenced by the way in which we commonly speak of the emotions as 'overwhelming' us, 'surging over' us, or 'taking possession of' us. Now, if we limit ourselves to this way of thinking about the emotions it is natural to conclude that when our behaviour is emotionally motivated we cannot be acting freely. But such a view can only be supported by a specious assimilation of emotions to sensations. Thus statements about emotions are thought of as reports that one is experiencing certain sensations; for example, to say that I feel sympathetic towards someone would be to report a particular sensation which I have somehow observed myself to be experiencing. Since we talk about bodily sensations, like feeling sick, in similar ways, we conclude that the experiences emotion words name force themselves upon us in an analogous manner. This leads to the view that to say that one 'ought' to be sympathetic towards others does not make sense or at least to the view that such an 'ought' is not being used in the same sense as the 'ought' in, say, 'You ought to pay your debts.' We can only tell someone that he 'ought' to do something or be something when he is presumed to have some choice in the matter; and when it comes to sympathizing there can be no such freedom. But once we get away from this Cartesian assimilation of emotions to sensations and realize that, whatever else emotion words are used for, they are not only, or even largely, used to report involuntary sensations, we can recognize the possibility that some emotionally motivated behaviour can be just as free as any other and that therefore there can be no objection on such a ground to the suggestion that we 'ought' to be sympathetic towards others in the same way as we 'ought' to pay our debts and keep our promises.

Really two questions can be distinguished here. The first is: 'Can I choose to act out of an emotion?' The second: 'Can I choose to have an emotion in the first place?' Now, there is no doubt that we can choose whether to show, in our words and behaviour, such emotions as anger and fear. Similarly with sympathy. I may deliberately choose to keep my sympathetic inclinations in check or I may deliberately choose to act upon them.

We can temper the expression of our emotions in accordance with the circumstances; in Adam Smith's words, 'flatten . . . the sharpness of [our emotion's] natural tone, in order to reduce it to harmony and concord with the emotions of those about [us]' (*T.M.S.*, p. 275). However, I think that one could go further than this to say that not only can one choose whether or not to act out of a particular emotion but also, with some emotions at least, can one choose to feel the emotion itself. Now, with some emotions such as fear and anger, it sounds odd to talk as if one can choose to experience them. If someone said that he 'decided' to be frightened by X or angry at Y, you would probably be justified in thinking that he was not 'really' frightened or angry. But this does not necessarily seem to be the case with all emotions. Much, although not all, discourse consists of individuals trying, overtly or covertly, to persuade each other to their own way of thinking in relation to the subject of discussion. Suppose that I set about trying to influence my neighbour's opinion of a third person, Smith. I know my neighbour's tough and tender spots; and I can play upon these, emphasizing certain aspects of Smith's behaviour and background whilst suppressing certain others. If my performance is well-calculated and my neighbour hasn't much first-hand acquaintance with Smith himself, I may succeed in, say, destroying Smith the pillar of society and putting in its place Smith the subversive anarchist: respect will turn to hatred and disgust. The point I am trying to make is that if I can deliberately set out to influence or prompt someone else's emotions in such a fashion (and succeed), can I not do the same thing with myself? Here I think that we must distinguish between the question of training the emotions over a long time and the question of choosing to experience an emotion on a particular occasion. There is no doubt that we can train both ourselves and others to feel certain emotions rather than others and that in this sense it is possible to cultivate emotional dispositions. This is an extremely important part of the process of education understood in the broadest possible sense.[1] More than this, I should want to say, on the model just described, that by emphasizing some aspects of a situation and playing down others we can come to feel certain

---

[1] For the education of emotional dispositions see *Introduction to Moral Education* by John Wilson, Norman Williams, and Barry Sugarman. Of special interest is their concept of 'EMP'—'an awareness or insight into one's own and other people's feelings' (p. 192). See also John Macmurray's *Reason and Emotion* (*passim*).

emotions which we should otherwise not feel. This is particularly true in the case of sympathy. By bringing home to myself as forcibly as I can another's condition and by not dwelling on those factors which from experience I know might make me less concerned (such as the other's unpleasant character) I can go out of my way to sympathize with someone. In this context Hume's notion of adopting a general point of view untouched by my own interests and contingent circumstances is particularly appropriate. I think we are justified in concluding that not only can we cultivate our emotions so as to form certain emotional habits or dispositions but that we can also, in the case of sympathy at least, exercise some kind of choice in the matter of whether or not we experience a particular emotion. Sympathy, in particular, does not assume a passive, involuntary agent.

Objection (c) attributed to the Kantian position was that if moral worth were tied to the emotions then, since emotional capacity varies from individual to individual and is innately determined, it follows that it would come more naturally to some people than others to behave morally. Nature has not implanted the same quantity of sympathy in each man's heart. If we happen to be of a generous and sympathetic disposition, so much the better, says Kant; if, though, we happen to be 'cold in temperament and indifferent to the sufferings of others' (loc. cit.), this is to be regretted, he says, but we cannot do anything about it. He insists that neither state of affairs makes it any easier or harder for us to act morally: this is the crux of his attitude towards the emotions. Thus Kant would disagree profoundly with Bernard Williams's comment:

No human characteristic which is relevant to degrees of moral esteem can escape being an empirical characteristic, subject to empirical conditions, psychological history, and individual variation, whether it be sensitivity, persistence, imaginativeness, intelligence, good sense; or sympathetic feeling; or strength of will. (*Morality and the Emotions*, pp. 23–4.)

For from Kant's point of view the unique importance of rationality lies in the fact that it *does* escape being such an empirical characteristic. Since I am not in a position to venture a critical appraisal of Kant's complete moral system I shall not pursue this line any further except to remind the reader of the frequent charge levelled against it that it is too formal and empty and although it forbids us from doing some things it cannot specifically encourage us to do anything in particular. Instead, I want to concentrate on what can be said on behalf of the emotions. The most important point immediately raised is that it is an open question just to what extent an individual is at a disadvantage when it comes to acting morally if morality and emotion were to be closely connected. Clearly, individuals' emotional capacities do vary greatly; but this means neither that they are determined innately nor that they cannot be deliberately cultivated. That we are virtually powerless to guide purposefully and creatively the emotional development of ourselves and others is a belief which can be seen reflected in much of our everyday thought about the nature of education. So people tend to think of education as a process which does, and perhaps can only, concentrate on developing the capacity for logical thought and its expression rather than on realizing such qualities as tolerance, sensitivity, and sympathy.[1] I should guess that if ever a position were reached where education was ordinarily seen equally in terms of the growth of intellectual skills *and* personal qualities then this would indicate that our prejudice against admitting moral value to at least some emotional dispositions was beginning to crumble away.

We are now in a position to review the full force of the arguments mustered against the view that the emotions have a positive part to play in the moral discourse. Despite their initial plausibility, none of them tell the whole story. Although some emotionally motivated conduct is capricious, there would seem to be a case for saying that sympathetic conduct, at least, can be principled and consistent. Further, if it is true that some emotions 'happen to us', it still makes sense to say that in the case of some at least (including sympathy) not only are we free to choose whether or not we shall be motivated by them but also are we free to choose whether or not we experience them in the first place. Finally, if it is true that we can cultivate or suppress emotional dispositions and habits then this means that people are not going to be irrevocably handicapped by their 'natural' emotional make-ups. The Kantian notion of emotion is a restricted one; it is not so much that the facts upon which these three objections have been based are untrue as that they present us with only half the picture.

[1] John Wilson (op. cit., pp. 448–58) discusses possible educational contexts specifically designed to encourage the development of these and other 'moral skills'.

To say that sympathy possesses moral value is not to say that
sympathy possesses this value unconditionally. Scheler suggests
in *The Nature of Sympathy* that the moral value of sympathy varies
according to (a) the appropriateness of the feelings of the person
sympathized with and (b) the value of this person himself. He
says:

   . . . the total value of an act of fellow-feeling varies according to the
worth of the value-situation which is the occasion of the other person's
sorrow or joy. In other words, to sympathize with joys and sorrows
which are appropriate to their circumstances is preferable to sympathizing with those which are not. By the same token, it is better to have
sympathy for a person of superior worth than for someone of lesser
value. (*N.S.*, p. 138.)

I do not think there is much to be said about this rather odious
suggestion except to point out that it is just not borne out by
common experience. It is considered just as valuable to sympathize with someone whose fears or anxieties are ill-founded as
with someone whose fears or anxieties are well-founded; and just
as valuable to sympathize with the degenerate as with the virtuous.

We can now move on to consider the second of the two theses
I mentioned at the outset of this chapter, namely, that sympathetic
action, the action prompted by sympathy, is *prima facie* right and
desirable action. This suggestion is compatible both with the
proposition that some sympathetic actions are not right and with
the proposition that right actions, if they are to be such, are not
necessarily sympathetic actions. Now sympathy entails a disposition to help the other person; and therefore sympathetic
action necessarily aims at, although it need not achieve, helping
the other person. So long as we bear in mind the distinction
between helping and assisting, it is clear that in itself it is always
desirable to help another person. Helping may involve either the
performance or the omission of certain actions; but in neither
case does it follow that what one does will be morally acceptable
from every point of view. By far the majority of sympathetic
actions which are considered wrong are so on the grounds that
they conflict with the requirements of justice, in one sense or
other. Thus it would be wrong to shelter a criminal out of sympathy either for him or for his family or to neglect special responsibilities we have undertaken because we sympathize with someone.
The extent and depth of our immediate sympathy for another is
governed by such factors as our particular relationship with him,

our own interests, and so on. If we acted according to our immediate sympathetic promptings there would be a great deal more partisanship in the world than there is already. It is clear that the bias arising both from this and the conflicting aims of individuals calls for some principle of impartiality. Our partial sympathetic tendencies have to be tempered by paying due regard to this demand. The clash between the sympathetic action and the just action is heightened by the fact that sympathy is concerned with the well-being of individuals whilst justice aims at that abstraction, the well-being of society, and because of this may, on particular occasions, be rendering no individual any good at all. In practice, this means that no matter how one's system of justice is organized, individuals will have to suffer in order that the very institution survive. On many occasions this is the sole justification for condemning the sympathetic action.

A further qualification can be added to this thesis. Sympathetic action is not right merely because it happens not to be in conflict with the notion of fairness, the law, or the agent's special responsibilities; more than this, it is necessary that the agent himself realize that his action is not in any such conflict. Before helping someone out of sympathy for him, it is essential (on this view) that the agent should have reflected as to the propriety of the help he intends. Suppose that a doctor is so sympathetic towards a particular patient that he devotes the whole of his consulting period to this man and that consequently a number of his patients receive no attention from him at all. In such a case we should say that, although the doctor's sympathy was desirable in itself, that it led him to neglect his other patients was most undesirable. But suppose that there were, as it happened, no other patients waiting to see the doctor that day. Our opinion of his behaviour would then turn on whether he knew this fact: if he did then we should have to retract our condemnation; if he did not then it would stand. I think that this example illustrates the point that if a person is to be said to have acted, in the case of sympathy, with any degree of moral discrimination, it is necessary that he must have been aware of, and considered, the possibility that his behaviour might be in conflict with some rational moral principle. It is not necessary, though, that on each separate occasion we should deliberate; we generalize and it is enough in many cases that we should have previously weighed up the pros and cons of acting sympathetically in such-and-such a kind of situation. But although very necessary, such generalization can be taken only so far; many situations cannot be anticipated and prescriptions cannot be given dogmatically. For example, it is widely assumed that if an act discriminates in favour of a few then this is an overwhelmingly good reason for it to be avoided. I am inclined to agree with Bernard Williams that this way of thinking exhibits what he calls a 'certain moral woodenness' (*Morality and the Emotions*, p. 22). After all, the principle of justice (in whatever sense it is developed) says nothing about *how* people should be treated apart from the fact that they should be treated, in one sense or other, equally. Merely because we are in a position to help some and not all is not necessarily a good reason for supposing that we should refrain from helping even those we can. But the point to emphasize is that in evaluating the sympathetic action not only do we consider whether or not it harmonizes with the requirements of justice but also whether or not this harmony was sheer chance.

To sum up the point we have reached. I have considered separately the questions of what value can be ascribed to sympathy as a motive and what value can be ascribed to the sympathetic action. Thus I have been principally concerned with showing, as against the Kantian position, that the emotions are far from being morally neutral and that sympathy at least possesses positive moral value. My argument has taken the form of indicating how it is possible for conduct to be both sympathetic and subject to reflection and deliberation. The Kantian arguments against admitting any moral worth to emotionally motivated conduct have been revealed as precariously balanced on a concept of emotion which assimilates emotions to sensations. My main conclusions are as follows. (a) As a motive or conative attitude towards another person, sympathy is unconditionally valuable. (b) In so far as we are free both to cultivate the capacity for conative sympathy and on particular occasions to exercise this capacity, it makes sense to say that we 'ought' to sympathize with others. (c) Sympathetic action is *prima facie* right and desirable action; that is, it is right and desirable so long as it does not clash with what may be termed the requirements of justice and so long as the agent realizes this fact.

We are now able to consider the final subject of this chapter, namely the question how far sympathy is a valid substitute for conscientiousness. Is it possible that one could guide one's life solely in accordance with a principle of sympathy—that is, without any appeal to a principle of duty? We shall have to approach this question rather obliquely.

Suppose that one asked why the need for consistency in moral conduct should be interpreted as the requirement that conduct, if it is to be morally valuable, should be inspired by one motive only. Kant would isolate the moral motive from all other—merely 'pathological'—motives. If a particular action is determined by a mixture of motives then it cannot possess moral value; since for the action to possess such value the motive for duty would have to be sufficiently strong *by itself* to prompt the agent to perform it. Now against this, one could suggest that if I help another because I recognize it to be my duty I act morally and that if I help him because I sympathize with him I also act morally; in other words, that moral value is not tied exclusively to the one motive or the other. By this I do not mean that all that matters is that one does the right action irrespective of the motive for doing it, but rather that there is more than one motive which possesses moral value. Immediately comes the objection that moral value is tied to obligation and praise and blame: if it is supposed to be good to act out of sympathy then we 'ought' to be sympathetic and if we are not we are to be 'blamed'. If we cannot say that we 'ought' to be sympathetic in exactly the same way as we 'ought' to do our duty (and despite my foregoing arguments there must always remain some cases where one would have to acknowledge that someone was just incapable of genuinely sympathizing with a particular person) then it looks as if we cannot maintain that sympathy has moral value. I would answer this objection by saying that on an occasion when one is incapable of sympathy one can always do the sympathetic thing not for the sake of duty but for the sake of sympathy. I shall try to spell this out. The injunction 'You ought to sympathize with your neighbour' can be understood as meaning that you ought to do the sympathetic thing by your neighbour, that is, what you would do if you were sympathetic but which you can now only do out of respect for your duty. There is clearly no difficulty about blaming a person for not being sympathetic in this sense. But is it really the case that we are left saying: 'It's a pity that you're not really sympathetic but you ought to do the sympathetic thing for the sake of duty'? Could we not instead demand: 'You ought to help this man either out of genuine sympathy for him or for the sake of sympathy'? Whichever was your motive your action would be externally the same; but in the first case your motive would be genuine sympathetic feeling whilst in the second it would be the recognition that what you were doing was the sympathetic thing. One could add, furthermore, that when one was able to act out of genuine sympathy one would not be acting, so to speak, blindly, since one would invariably recognize that what one was doing was the sympathetic thing. To act on this injunction, then, would be to act on the principle of sympathy. In so far as acting on such a principle of sympathy always involves, although not necessarily as a motive, the recognition of what in the circumstances would be the sympathetic thing to do, it is distinct from acting immediately from sympathetic feelings. Further, in so far as to act on such a principle obviates the need for reference to a principle of duty, it is open to suggest that it would be perfectly possible for someone, at least with regard to the virtue of beneficence, to regulate *without appeal to duty* that part of his life which impinges on others. In other words, at least in the case of beneficence, sympathy could be considered as a legitimate substitute for conscientiousness.

Although to point out that sympathy is morally valuable does not imply that one cannot accord some (or even a special kind of) value to conscientiousness, it does mean that not all value belongs to conscientiousness and that consequently it cannot be the supreme moral motive which Kant would have us believe it to be. To exalt conscientiousness as the supreme virtue is to miss its point—which is to act as a *substitute* for the 'natural virtues', sympathy among them. Hume recognizes this very clearly in the *Treatise* in his account of the relation between 'the sense of duty' and the 'natural virtues'. We can only feel obliged to do something out of a sense of duty if we can have a natural inclination to do it anyway:

Tho' there was no obligation to relieve the miserable, our humanity wou'd lead us to it; and when we omit that duty, the immorality of the omission arises from its being a proof, that we want the natural sentiments of humanity. A father knows it to be his duty to take care of his children: But he has also a natural inclination to it. And if no human creature had that inclination, no one cou'd lie under any such obligation. (*Treatise*, p. 518.)

P. H. Nowell-Smith makes essentially the same point in *Ethics*:

The so-called 'natural virtues' are dispositions to do certain sorts of things towards which we have, in general, a pro-attitude; and moral rules are rules enjoining these same things. Hence the conscientious man will do exactly the same thing a man with all the natural virtues will do. He does not do them for the same reason; and he is not brave or honest or kindly, since he acts for the sake of doing his duty, not for the sake of doing the brave or honest or kindly thing. But he will do what the brave, honest and kindly man does. (*Ethics*, p. 258.)

To see, then, conscientiousness as a substitute for natural virtue brings out two important things. First, it indicates the absurdity of denying the value of that for which conscientiousness is a substitute. Even if conscientiousness and the natural virtues are valuable in different ways, or are measured on two different scales of value, this is no reason for supposing that conscientiousness alone should possess specifically *moral* value. Secondly, it shows that it is in its capacity to motivate a man to perform the same actions that a man with all the natural virtues would be moved to do that the unique, though not supreme, value of conscientiousness lies.[1] That conscientiousness is a substitute in this sense is further borne out by the vaguely formulated but, I think, widely held view that the *really* good man is the man who *wants* to do what is good and avoid what is evil and who consequently does not see the moral law as an imperative. Reference to this view helps to explain why Kant's notion of a Holy Will seems so far removed from the experience of ordinary moral thinking. According to Kant, what a perfectly good will or Holy Will wills is necessarily in harmony with the moral law. There can be no imperatives for a Holy Will. For such a will the notion of obligation has no reference. (See *G.M.M.*, p. 81.) But if a Holy Will *must* will the good then it has no choice; and if it has no choice it is hard to see how it could possess moral value in the same sense as imperfect (human) wills may do when they act out of respect for

[1] A popular but muddled idea is perhaps worth mentioning in this context. This is that it is both difficult and unenjoyable to act virtuously and that since it cannot be difficult to act naturally one cannot be acting virtuously when one is acting naturally. There seem to be at least three confusions here. (a) 'It is easy to be "natural".' But the word 'natural' is notoriously ambiguous: it may well be as easy to make a pig of oneself as it is difficult to be genuinely sympathetic—but both are natural' ways of behaving. The seed of sympathy is there in the first place; but we have to cultivate it. (b) 'What is difficult is not enjoyable and therefore it cannot be enjoyable to be virtuous.' The premiss is untrue. Aristotle believed that a man was not really good unless he *enjoyed* doing what was good. (c) A third mistake is to confuse the psychological penumbra which contingently accompanies doing the virtuous thing with what it is that makes the virtuous thing virtuous. Against this, we can say that although it may be difficult to act conscientiously, this difficulty is not part of what it is to be conscientious.

the moral law. By contrast, with the sympathetic man (that is, the man directly motivated by sympathy) there is no question of his *having* to do what he does. When we act out of sympathy there is no sense in which we are necessitated to do what we do. The saint does what he does because he wants to, not because he thinks he ought to do what he thinks is his duty. None of us are saints and for this reason conscientiousness is the special virtue of human beings. But in so far as it is possible to have saintly aspirations and ideals, these are not to be described in terms of acting for the sake of duty.

VII

SYMPATHY AS THE PRECONDITION
OF MORALITY

As a conative attitude towards another person, sympathy is always good. But the action it inspires is only conditionally good; that is, although it is not necessarily the case that all sympathetic action has moral value or that all morally valuable behaviour is sympathetic, it nevertheless always makes sense to ask of a particular sympathetic action whether it is right or wrong. This then in brief is the answer I have suggested to the question of whether or not moral value can be ascribed to sympathy. But to take up a different question now, in what sense can one say that morality is *based* on sympathy? The respective attempts of Hume and Smith to explain the nature of moral evaluation in terms of sympathy have each proved unsatisfactory. I think we are now in a position to suggest a more fruitful approach to the question. From the theses which I put forward in the previous chapter it is still open for someone to hold that to have a capacity for sympathy is not a necessary condition of being a moral agent. It could be argued that, as motives for moral conduct, sympathy and conscientiousness were mutual alternatives; that they reflected two logically self-contained ways of life. The conscientious man and the sympathetic man would be considered as good as each other. We might prefer the one man to the other, the one way of life to the other, but this would be just a matter of taste and of no moral significance. The important assumption in this kind of view is that a man devoid of sympathy could lead a moral—as opposed to a non-moral—life. Against such a view, I think we can advance a thesis which connects sympathy and morality in a way quite distinct from any already suggested. This new thesis is independent of, and does not stand or fall by the success of, those of the previous chapter. It would hold that *sympathy is a necessary precondition of morality*; in other words, that to be a moral agent presupposes a capacity for sympathy of some kind. If we can point to concepts which form a necessary part of moral discourse and which are conceptually dependent on sympathy then this would provide evidence in favour of this new thesis. With this end in mind then, I want to discuss the logical relations which hold between the notion of sympathy and in particular the notions of beneficence, respect for persons as such, obligation to others, and justice. I do not mean to suggest by this choice that morality can be reduced into terms of these particular concepts and no others. But it does seem reasonable to suppose that an under-standing of what it is to help others, to value people intrinsically, to have obligations to others, and to be just, is necessary if one is to be considered a moral being, that is, a being capable of acting and thinking with some degree of moral discrimination. First of all, then, I wish to discuss sympathy and beneficence.

We frequently help others out of the motive of conscientious-ness; that is, we help them not because we are naturally inclined to help them but because we think it is our duty to help them. On such occasions conscientiousness proves its worth as a substitute for 'natural virtue'. But the question is whether it would be possible for us to help others consistently and at all times only because we thought it was our duty to do so. That is, is it logically possible? Is Kantian Man a logical possibility? Professor Acton, for one, thinks not and in principle I agree with him. I now want to consider in some detail his argument as it appears in 'The Ethical Importance of Sympathy' (*Philosophy*, 1955).

Roughly speaking, Acton's main contention in this paper is that the occasions on which we help others out of conscientious-ness or out of regard for some rational principle are parasitic on those occasions on which we help others out of sympathy. It is therefore impossible to act for the sake of duty *all the time*. Although on a particular occasion we may help another out of regard for some purely rational principle, this 'present rational act is, as it were, an extension or revival of . . . past sympathetic ones' ('E.I.S.', p. 62). Acton's argument in support of this view appears to be as follows. Only creatures which experience needs can be helped. We cannot describe what it would be like for a purely rational creature to have a need; and therefore we have to discount the possibility that such a being could be said to help another such being. Therefore, only creatures with feelings and needs can be helped. Furthermore, they can only be helped by creatures similar to themselves; that is, creatures also possessing feelings and needs. A purely rational being would not know what it was to help a sentient being. Such a being could conceivably be instructed on how to benefit a creature with needs and feelings; but even if, on the strength of these instructions, he could set about successfully improving this sentient creature's condition he could not be said to have *helped* him. He would be parasitic on his instructor.

He would know only part of what [other people] meant when they asked for help, for he would not understand *why* they wanted to change their present situation. His attitude towards other people's hunger and thirst, for example, would be more like that of a mechanic towards an engine running out of fuel than that of a man towards another man in trouble. ('E.I.S.', p. 62.)

Since such a rational being could not fully understand what it is to experience a need it follows that he cannot fully understand why he ought to do something about it. And therefore he 'could not have full insight into the moral significance of his deeds, but would be mechanically carrying out a principle he had received from others, or *automatically* conforming to a law of his own rational nature' ('E.I.S.', p. 63). It follows that I can only help a person out of conscientiousness or a regard for some rational principle in so far as in the past I have sympathized with other people in situations similar to the present one. Therefore, in so far as morality consists of helping others it must presuppose sympathy. If we cannot be moral unless we can help others (as opposed to merely ameliorating their condition) then, since helping implies sympathy, it follows that we cannot be considered capable of morally significant acts if we have no capacity for sympathy.

A second point, distinct from the one set out above, which Acton makes is that

a certain amount of sympathy is required if anyone is even to *notice* that someone else is *in need* of help, for, it might be said, it is under the stimulus of fellow-feeling that an objective or contemplative attitude is transformed into a sensitive awareness of ways in which they may be helped or harmed and have a moral claim upon our services. ('E.I.S.', p. 62.)

But he does not develop this theme further.

Acton's main argument seems to prove more than he intends it to. For it seems to prove that not only a purely rational being acting on purely rational principles could not help a sentient being but also that a sentient being acting on a particular occasion on a purely rational principle such as conscientiousness could not be truly said to help another sentient being. I shall try to explain this. Acton suggests that an act performed only out of regard for a rational principle can be seen as an 'extension or revival' of past sympathetic acts.

> We may therefore say that although he does not at present sympathize with the man whom he is helping, he once sympathized with men in similar situations so that his present rational act is, as it were, an extension or revival of his past sympathetic ones. ('E.I.S.', p. 62.)

The implication is that in this respect the agent may still be thought of as *helping* the other person. But the 'as it were' seems to mask a weakness in the argument. It is not altogether clear wherein the difference lies between the act of someone whose personal griefs on a particular occasion render him unable to feel with others but who acts as he ought to and the act of a purely rational being 'automatically conforming to a law of his own nature' or acting on the instructions of a third party. *Ex hypothesi* they each act out of regard for a rational principle. So, on what grounds can one hold that the first agent is *helping* the other person whilst the second is at best merely alleviating distress? Acton correctly points out that for someone to help another out of trouble he must be able to see why the other person needs to be helped, why he wants a change in his condition. But if this is so then he seems to be wrong in assuming that a person even temporarily 'unable to feel with others' can '*help* them as he ought'. He is wrong because such a person *ex hypothesi* would be unable to see why the other's condition ought to be changed since he would be unable to sympathize with him at all. The conclusion which Acton should have strictly reached, then, is that when we act out of regard for a rational principle such as duty we can never be said to be, in the fullest sense, helping others—even though there may be other occasions on which we give help purely out of sympathy. In other words, whether conscientiousness has *any* moral value at all would be called into question.

This view seems just as unpalatable as Kant's. But there is a good chance of rehabilitation. The first thing which can be pointed out is that in any case beneficence is not the whole of morality; consequently, the value of conscientious action in the realm of, say, justice is not questioned by this argument even if it were correct. The second is that the conclusion that help offered out of conscientiousness cannot possess the same moral significance that help offered out of sympathy does can be avoided if we take up Acton's subsidiary point that a certain amount of sympathy is necessary if one is even to notice that another person needs help. I think that there are two reasons why Acton's argument goes astray : he does not clarify what he means by 'sympathy'; and he does not clearly mark off the occasions when he is using sympathy as a motive for helping from the occasions when he is using sympathy as a logical precondition of helping. What is it that makes an act specifically an act of helping? It is certainly not the motive; for we can help others from all manner of motives, some good and some bad. Rather, two things appear to characterize an act as helping: (a) that the agent's object or aim is to improve, in some way or other, another's condition; and (b) that the agent realizes that the other person needs help. As Acton recognizes, this second factor calls for a certain amount of sympathy from the agent. But this sympathy need only be fellow-feeling, not active sympathy. If these two conditions are fulfilled then whatever the motive, whether it be conscientiousness, fear, spite, self-interest, or sympathy, the agent can truly be said to be helping the other person. A limiting case will be the act performed by a purely rational being—it could not fulfil the second condition. But the rational act of a sentient being temporarily unable to sympathize will not be excluded. Now Acton said that the present rational act of a sentient being is to be considered as 'an extension or revival of past sympathetic acts'. The essence of his view is that there is a difference between the act of a rational being and the rational act of a sentient being and that this difference lies in the capacity for sympathy which the latter possesses. But he does not explain how this capacity for sympathy makes a difference.

Now it seems that before one can have a motive for helping someone one has to have realized the possibility or appropriateness of giving help to that person in that situation. This very realization that help is appropriate relies on a sympathetic understanding of the situation; a recognition, in other words, that the situation *needs* changing because another person is *in need*. But to say that sympathy is required for the agent to see that another needs help is not to say anything about the motive for giving that help; and he may decide to help out of conscientiousness, out of sympathy, or out of self-interest, or, perhaps more likely, out of a mixture of all these and other motives. Now the 'sympathy' I have suggested is a necessary part of helping is not active sympathy but rather 'sympathy' understood as passive fellow-feeling. Although active sympathy is impossible without this more primitive level of sympathy, the former is not necessarily implied by the latter. (Acton talks just of 'sympathy'.) So we are now in a position to say that a purely rational being cannot be said to help a sentient being; for in order to help, an agent must realize that another person needs help; and this realization requires at least fellow-feeling with the other. Sympathy as fellow-feeling is thus the logical precondition of helping. But even though the agent has fellow-feeling his motive for helping the other person may yet be a regard for some purely rational principle. If, then, one wants to deny moral value to acts aimed at alleviating distress but motivated by a sense of duty, one is not entitled to do so on the ground that one cannot be said to help another when one is acting solely out of regard for a rational principle. Acton states ambiguously that only help 'based on sympathy with the sufferer' ('E.I.S.', p. 64) receives moral approval. But what does he mean here by 'based'? Faced by the obvious fact that conscientious acts of helping *do* receive moral approval, he is driven to the position of having to say that such conscientious acts somehow get their warrant from sympathetic acts in the agent's past. By distinguishing between the two senses of 'sympathy' and between the meaning of 'helping' and the motive for helping, I hope to have clarified the claim that sympathy underlies beneficence. Although sympathy as fellow-feeling is a logical precondition of helping others, it is still true that the motive for helping may be sympathy as practical concern *or* a regard for a rational principle such as conscientiousness.

A separate point which Acton does not mention but which seems worth drawing attention to is the extent to which sympathy affects the *nature* of our help. There are appropriate and inappropriate ways of helping others, and it seems natural to suppose that the more fully we sympathize with someone the more likely we are to give him the kind of help he needs. In many cases this will be to treat him as he wants to be treated—but not necesssarily, for not everyone knows all the time what is best for himself. Misguided or inappropriate help seems to be due to the agent's own restricted experience or to his limited imagination or to a plain lack of effort of imagination. Again, this is more a question of fellow-feeling than of active sympathy. Suppose that I realize that someone needs help but that beyond this I cannot sympathize with him because I am preoccupied with my own personal anxieties; nevertheless, because I see it is my duty to help him I do so. In such a case there does not seem to be any reason why I should not know how to help the other person even though I do not actively sympathize with him. To recognize that a person is in need is to recognize how he may be helped. It still remains true, though, that the more closely we go along with the other person and the more closely we can share in his situation, the greater the likelihood of our help being acceptable and/or appropriate. There is always a danger of stereotyping other people's needs. Moreover, not only does sympathy affect the precise nature of the help given but also the *way* in which it is given. To be given charity is often a humiliating experience—not lessened by the attitude of the charitable body itself. To be surprised if one's beneficiaries are not grateful for the charity they have been given indicates a lack of sympathetic understanding.

To be given charity is humiliating when one is obviously thought of as an *object* of charity. People often refuse charity on the grounds that they would 'lose' their self-respect if they accepted it: perhaps it would be nearer the truth to say that they would be *denied* it. It depends on how the charity is given. If we actively sympathize with someone then we cannot treat him as an object, as an instrument for our own self-satisfaction; on the contrary, we see him as a being possessing individual worth and existing in his own right. It is this *respect for persons as such* which I now want to move on to discuss.

Conative sympathy is partial; although we could say that through sympathy we see that others count, we do not see that they should all count equally. But although justice is an important concept for morality it is at the same time a restricted concept. To say that people ought to be treated 'justly' or 'impartially' or 'equally' or 'fairly' is to specify how they should be treated only in relation to one another. That is, justice deals only with the *relative* worth of individuals. To be just is not to prefer this man to that man or, if we treat one man in a particular way, to treat the remainder in the same way. But this is not to say that men possess any intrinsic worth: to hold that all individuals or all individuals belonging to a particular class according to their possession of certain characteristics should be treated on the same footing is quite compatible with the view that as individuals they possess no intrinsic worth at all. It is clear, then, that the working use of the principle of justice presupposes that individuals *qua* individuals do possess value.

Furthermore, there are situations which may be designated 'moral' in which an appeal to impartiality or fairness is inappropriate. It is no accident that by 'justice' we tend to think of *legal* justice, as something to be dispensed by courts and judges; for justice requires a third party. But it is a mistake to think of the judicial situation as the paradigm moral situation. (Indeed, it is a mistake to look for a 'paradigm moral situation'.) Certainly there are occasions on which a consideration of what would be just and what would be unjust is the only one which matters; when, for instance, we are in the position of referees or legislators. But probably the most common, and usually what seem the most urgent and perplexing, are those situations in which we ourself are one of the participants. These are what we could call 'self–other' situations. And justice and impartiality do not seem to be the appropriate concepts to bring to bear on this kind of situation. Suppose that I and another man are on an expedition across the Sahara and we reach a stage when there is not enough water for both of us to survive: if we share the water we are both bound to die but if one of us has all the water then he may possibly reach safety. All other things being equal, what ought I to do? The only answer to such a riddle is to point out that you cannot categorically say what one ought to do in this or any such situation. If I appeal to the principle of impartiality then we should share the water. On the other hand, it could be argued that since I ought to prefer others to myself my companion should have the water. Neither course of action would be open to moral censure. There are two ways of looking at the problem: the just act, though moral, is not the only moral act. In a given situation we should not insist that there is always only one act which 'ought' to be done. Take another example. I am a rich man. A poor man owes me money. If I take what I am entitled to I should leave him penniless. Now suppose that I feel like putting my money to better purpose. From the judicial point of view I can justify my claim; after all, it is my money, I can say, and I've a perfect right to have it back whenever I choose. But in reply, we can point out that I am really only rationalizing my behaviour and that although it can be seen to be justified from one point of view there are other points of view from which it cannot be justified. If one insists on one's pound of flesh then one is sidestepping the real issue. This is that it is *I* who am involved—*I* in relation to another person. The judicial point of view is far from identical with the moral point of view. To quote W. G. Maclagan:

> The moral principle of impartiality, then, is ultimate for the framing and execution of law, and for moral action generally so far, but *only* so far, as it is analogous to this; which is to say, so far only as it concerns our treatment of one person other than ourselves in relation to another person other than ourselves. It does not govern the treatment of others in relation to ourselves. ('R.P.M.P.', p. 197.)

A stickler for the letter of the law may not be truly carrying out his responsibilities as a human being; he may well be guilty of bad faith.

The concept of justice is therefore neither appropriate to the 'self–other' situation nor does it accredit any intrinsic worth to persons as such. Maclagan suggests that the concept which exhibits both these characteristics which are lacking in justice is that of the principle of respect for persons as such. Further, he suggests that the principle of respect is intimately connected with the notion of *agape* and that sympathy underlies both the principle of respect and *agape*. The latter are both 'moralized' forms of sympathy. The interesting thing is the nature of the relation which is supposed to exist between sympathy on the one hand and respect and *agape* on the other. But before examining this relation, we have to be clear as to what Maclagan understands by respect and *agape*.

The principle of respect for persons as such implies that an individual *qua* individual has value. Even if there were two individuals in every respect identical they would each possess separate worth in virtue of their individuality. The principle of respect is not interested in what people are *like*; it is merely interested in their being people. To respect a person as such is to treat him as an end in himself. The ultimate denial of the principle of respect would be to treat another as a mere instrument, as a slave. Now in its attention to the being of a person rather than to what he is like, the principle of respect is akin to love; and if we distinguish between love as romantic, sexually tinged *eros* and love as *agape* then respect is more closely connected with the second than the first. Admittedly, the passion of *eros* is concerned with the being of the other and not with what he is like; but it falls short of the principle of respect in that it is in fact (though not ideally) changeable and in that it is exclusive, its object being this particular person and no other. But love understood as *agape* is neither capricious nor exclusive:

[In *agape*] we have that volitional 'set' appropriate to the adoption of a moral principle, incorporating the *positive* value of persons as such that underlies the *comparative* valuation involved in justice, and incorporating it in a form that is wholly outward-looking and that satisfies accordingly our sense that our moral concern is for others and is not impartially attentive to self and others alike. ('R.P.M.P.', p. 206.)

Agape, then, takes us beyond the scope of justice. It entails a positive, absolute valuation of our fellows as such. Although we cannot 'adopt' *agape* (being more aptly described as an emotional response than a principle) we can abstract from *agape* this notion of the absolute value of individuals and formulate it into a practical moral principle—the principle of respect for persons as such. *Agape* and the principle of respect are the opposite faces of the same coin. Exactly how this is so we shall be able to see once we have understood their relations to the concept of sympathy.

Maclagan distinguishes between 'animal sympathy' (that is, what I have called 'infection') and 'human sympathy'. The latter he divides into 'passive' and 'active'. 'Passive' sympathy is a fellow-feeling involving a consciousness of the subjectivity of another; whilst 'active' sympathy implies a practical concern for the other (that is, what I have called 'conative' sympathy). Maclagan describes this passive sympathy as the 'natural matrix' of active sympathy. But the active sympathy of practical concern is still to be distinguished from *agape* proper. According to Maclagan, active sympathy is unprincipled and still waits to be effectively moralized.

Active sympathy is transformed into *agape*, Maclagan suggests, by its fusion with 'our general consciousness of obligation'. *Agape* is thus to be analysed into two constituents; on the one hand purely natural sympathy and on the other a sense of obligation. These two factors are the preconditions of *agape*. This sense of obligation is brought into being by, in the first place, a realization of the difference between 'I ought' and 'I want', and in the second place, a sincere response to the challenge with which the gap between desire and obligation presents us. In so far as it 'moralizes' active sympathy the sense of obligation performs both a negative and a positive function. 'Its negative function is, primarily, to remove the psychological obstacle to *agape* that is created by our natural self-centredness and self-concern' ('R.P.M.P.', p. 210). The positive function of the sense of obligation is to advance the status of the other from that of '*natural* object of concern to that of *proper* object of concern' ('R.P.M.P.', p. 216). This moralized concern for the other is equivalent to the principle of respect for others as such. The principle of respect and *agape* are 'identical as regards their objective significance, their practical or directive import' but they are 'subjectively different' ('R.P.M.P.', p. 216). This difference lies in the fact that *agape*, being the moralized form of natural sympathy, carries with it a *warmth* of attitude which is not to be found in the principle of respect. Although the principle of respect is conceptually dependent on natural sympathy, in practice it is still possible to regulate one's conduct and attitudes towards others according to the principle of respect and without feeling sympathetic towards them.

Although without the warmth of personal sympathy we could never have understood and formulated the claim of persons to our practical respect, once we have done so we can adhere to the principle doggedly, in no merely routine and incomprehending manner, despite all the vicissitudes of feeling, and even when it would be at least natural to say that our feelings were dead. ('R.P.M.P.', p. 217.)

There is a possible objection to the argument that active sympathy provides us with the notion of respect for persons as such. It might be held that the notion of the intrinsic worth of persons is derived not from the experience of sympathy but from reflection on the rationality of the will. The directive import of Kant's formula of the end in itself seems to be identical with that of the principle of respect. A rational being is the only end in itself, the only thing capable of possessing absolute, unconditional value; consequently we should always act so as to treat humanity, whether it be in our own person or in that of another, as an end in itself. This unconditioned worth attaches to persons, according to Kant, in virtue of their rationality: 'Rational nature exists as an end in itself' (*G.M.M.*, p. 96). Against this objection, Maclagan suggests ('R.P.M.P.', p. 199) that strictly speaking the importance that attaches to the rational will belongs neither to the will itself nor to the person but to the *moral goodness* of which the will is the possible locus. If this were so then we could say that the will is only conditionally valuable—that is, conditional on its potentiality for good. If the worth of persons were derived from reflection on their potentiality to be Good Wills then if we supposed that 'some person's will was incurably corrupt, would it not be reasonable to acquiesce in the idea of the total obliteration of his being?' ('R.P.M.P.', p. 199). But if we did acquiesce in such an idea then it would only be with a bad conscience; and this would be an index of the inability to accept such an attitude as morally proper. If the above counter-argument of Maclagan's is correct then it follows that any value we attach to persons as rational wills is not so absolute as the value we attach to persons which is derived from, and logically dependent on, the notion of practical sympathy.

Not only beneficence and respect for persons as such but also the concept of moral obligation seems to be intimately connected with that of sympathy. Basically, an obligation is a relation which ties one being to another being. It is a relation which lacks logical symmetry: if X is to be obliged to Y about Q then X must understand what it is to have such a thing as an obligation to another even if he is unaware of the existence of this particular obligation Q; on the other hand, not only could it be possible for Y to be ignorant of X's obligation to him but also could it be possible for him not to understand what it is to have such an obligation. Just how do we characterize the class of beings to which it is logically possible to have an obligation? I suggest that in order for there to be the possibility of moral obligation the speaker (who is not necessarily the bearer of the obligation) must realize that there is another being possessing the capacity for feeling and suffering. It is impossible to talk about having obligations to, say, cars and houses, sticks and stones, since these things lack sensitivity. I should further suggest that it can only be through sympathy (passive if not active) that the speaker can grasp the meaning of 'the other', that is, become aware of the existence of another centre of consciousness similar to himself but not himself. What I want to say could be put by saying that sympathizing with another, either passively or actively, entails the possibility of having a moral obligation to the being with which you sympathize. When I assert that I sympathize with X then I tacitly acknowledge that I *could* have an obligation to X. If I can be obliged to X then X has the capacity to have a *claim* on me. Although X will possess the capacity to bear claims X does not have to be a conscious bearer of these claims. Thus we can have obligations to those who do not, and cannot, know that they have claims upon us, for instance, children, the mentally handicapped, animals, and other non-rational but sensitive beings. It is no coincidence that we recognize the possibility of having obligations only to those creatures with whom we recognize the possibility of sympathizing. In other words, our moral obligations extend as far as our capacity for sympathy extends. If we could sympathize with insects, trees, and stones then we could have moral obligations to them.

I have left until last the discussion of the relation between justice and sympathy because it seems to be the most problematical of the four relationships I have chosen. Fundamentally, justice implies impartiality or the demand that everyone should count for one and for no more than one. That justice presupposes sympathy seems hardly plausible, therefore. I have previously suggested that sympathy may show us that others count but not that they count either equally with each other or equally with ourselves; that is, others are not necessarily seen *on a par* with each other or with ourselves. 'Justice' can be broken down into more specific notions; we can make a distinction between distributive justice, corrective justice and commutative justice or fairness. Distributive justice may be organized on a basis of arithmetical equality or proportional equality. Arithmetical equality implies equal treatment for all, regardless of individual needs. Thus if I am to share a cake among four people I must give each exactly a quarter, irrespective of whether he likes cake, is hungrier, bigger, or smaller than his companions. This notion can be refined by pointing out that it is not just a question of equal treatment as such as much as a question of considering individuals' needs and giving equal treatment to equal needs, that is, a question of proportional equality. Understanding justice primarily in this sense, Professor Acton suggests that there is a connection between justice and sympathy:

> . . . it is clear that a being who is able to imagine himself in the place of another so as to realize the other's sufferings as if they were his own has achieved some measure of impartiality. The other man's suffering is not indifferent to him, but exerts a certain pressure for relief comparable with his own natural desire to relieve his own. The other man's distress is at least *comparable* with his, and the road has been opened up that leads to the demand for equal treatment of equal needs. ('E.I.S.', p. 66.)

It strikes me that the suggested connection is rather tenuous. What exactly is Acton claiming when he says that 'the road has been opened up that leads to the demand for equal treatment of equal needs'? The fact that another's distress is comparable with my own does not mean that when I do compare them I shall attach equal importance to the relief of the one as I do to the relief of the other. It is true that sympathy partially lifts us out of the egocentric position and informs us of the existence of other sentient beings; and also that on occasions sympathy will lead us to prefer others to ourselves; but to say these things is quite distinct from saying that sympathy shows us that we should consistently treat each of these beings on a par both with ourselves and with each other.

A similar but more specific claim to derive the principles of justice from sympathy or compassion is made by Schopenhauer in his essay *On the Basis of Morality*. Sympathy furnishes us with what he considers to be the basic maxim of justice, namely, 'Injure no man':

> ... the first degree of the effect of compassion is that it opposes and impedes those sufferings which I intend to cause to others by my inherent antimoral forces. It calls out to me 'Stop!'; it stands before the other man like a bulwark, protecting him from the injury that my egoism or malice would otherwise urge me to do. Thus there arises from this first degree of compassion the maxim *Neminem laede* [Injure no one], i.e., the fundamental principle of *justice*. (*On the Basis of Morality*, p. 149.)

Now the obvious objection to Schopenhauer's argument is that the maxim 'Injure no one' is *not* the fundamental principle of justice. If one had to formulate one then perhaps something like 'Treat everyone alike' would be more satisfactory. So long as we made no exceptions (including ourselves) we could with justice injure everyone. Moreover, it could be argued that there are some occasions where to injure an individual is to do the just thing and to do otherwise to act unjustly. Both Acton and Schopenhauer seem to be offering historical accounts of how the experience of sympathizing with others leads to the development of the idea of justice and what they say sheds only a little light on the logical connection between the two concepts.

Now in the discussion of beneficence I asked whether it were possible fully to understand what it was to help another without understanding what it was to sympathize with another. On this model, then, the question we should now be asking is whether it is possible to understand what it is to be just or impartial in one's treatment of others without knowing what it is to sympathize with others. I suggest that the short answer is in fact 'No'. The principal reason for maintaining that a being without sympathy could not have the full moral insight into the significance of what it was to help another was that such a being would be unable to appreciate *why* the other person's situation should be changed. In the present case, if we asked, on this analogy, whether a being without sympathy could give an adequate answer to the question why he should treat others impartially what kind of answer could he produce? I think it could only be in terms of demonstrating how impossible life would be without some principle of impartiality, that is, by reference to the chaos and anarchy of the 'state of nature' and so on. But no matter how filled out, such an answer could never be considered satisfactory because it fails to take into account that aspect of impartiality which makes us reluctant to approve of partiality even in circumstances where its practical consequences are trivial—namely, the belief that individuals qua individuals are *entitled* to equal treatment. If we take my earlier suggestion that the fundamental principle of justice could be expressed in the maxim 'Treat everyone alike' then the vital question has become 'Who is to count as "everyone"?'. Are children to be included? Foetuses? The insane? Animals? Plants? Machines? The answer we give will depend on which of these we feel we could sympathize with. If a person is to be said to be able to use such words as 'just' and 'impartial' properly he must be able to mention the kind of things which can be treated with or without justice and impartiality and distinguish them from the kind of things for which these concepts are inappropriate. But in deciding this question he cannot, I should say, choose any criterion arbitrarily. Consider the following sentences: 'He decided to treat everyone with black hair and blue eyes impartially' and 'Justice was given to everyone with an income of over £1,000 a year.' Such sentences sound decidedly self-contradictory and that they do is an index that the notions of justice and impartiality not only entail propositions about how everyone should be treated in relation to everyone else but also demand that 'everyone' should be understood as 'all sentient creatures'. It is nonsense to talk about 'treating machines impartially or justly'—for the simple reason that machines are not sentient creatures. Machines can be damaged, can function badly, and be repaired, but they cannot be harmed, suffer, or be helped. Clearly, there are disagreements about what does and does not count as a sentient creature entitled to be treated with impartiality—and these differences will reflect the different sympathetic capacities of those who disagree. My main point, then, is that a purely rational being without sympathy could not really be said to understand all that is involved in treating others justly or impartially because such a being could have no direct insight into the reason why it is impossible to treat a machine or any other inanimate object with justice or impartiality. Justice and impartiality, far from being concepts which can be applied arbitrarily to any class of beings, are applicable only to what I have called the class of sentient beings; and in so far as the notion of a sentient being can only be understood by reference to passive sympathy it follows that justice and impartiality are ultimately conceptually dependent on this kind of sympathy.

My arguments in this and the previous two chapters point to the following conclusions about sympathy and morality:

(1) Although in itself without any kind of moral value, infectious sympathy, in so far as it helps to explain the dissemination and standardization of particular beliefs, attitudes and feelings within a society, appears to be what can be termed a 'moralizing' force of great social importance.

(2) Passive sympathy or fellow-feeling is the logical precondition of the notions of beneficence or helping others, being morally obliged to others, and treating others with justice and impartiality. Active or conative sympathy is the logical precondition of the principle of respecting individuals *qua* individuals. It follows, then, that in so far as beneficence, obligation, respect, justice, and impartiality are all concepts fundamental to moral discourse, to be considered an agent capable of genuine moral discrimination and insight presupposes a capacity for sympathy, both active and passive.

(3) Contrary to the Kantian outlook, it can be justifiably claimed that conative sympathy as a possible motive for action possesses unconditional moral value and that the action this sympathy may prompt is *prima facie* right and desirable. I have argued that to act upon the principle of sympathy is equivalent to doing the sympathetic thing either because you genuinely sympathize or because you recognize it as the sympathetic thing to do. Moreover,

to act on such a principle is in many cases a morally viable alternative to acting out of conscientiousness. I should emphasize that this thoughtful, principled sympathy is not to be confused with the notion of *agape*—which is an emotional attitude permeating every dimension of a man's life. The cultivation of a sympathetic nature approaches, but can never be identical with, the condition of *agape*. It is impossible, for instance, to describe a person as someone who 'nearly always acts out of *agape*'. But this is just what is possible about conative sympathy, even when it is genuinely principled and thoughtful; and it is this feature which puts it realistically within the grasp of human beings. The fact that on a particular occasion a man acts without sympathy or fails to sympathize does not of itself mean that he is an unsympathetic man. There is room for lapses.

(4) Nevertheless, it is impossible to lead a life which is both truly moral and independent of either sympathy or duty. Whilst we could imagine a being which led an exclusively conscientious existence in the sense that all its conduct was directly regulated by the rational principle of doing what it recognized as its duty, such a being would be utterly unable to understand the moral significance of its behaviour—for the moral significance of the virtue of conscientiousness is parasitic on a capacity for sympathetic feeling. On the other hand, although it seems possible that a man could with true moral insight regulate the bulk of his life in so far as it impinges on those of others in accordance with what I have called 'the principle of sympathy', I think it is doubtful whether adhering solely to such a principle he could properly order his life in connection with matters of justice and impartiality. Both sympathy and duty are key concepts of different aspects of morality. In practice, in so much as we attempt to guide our lives in relation to other people's, this must be through an unanalysable mixture of, among many other things, sympathy *and* conscientiousness.

BIBLIOGRAPHY

ACTON, H. B., 'The Ethical Importance of Sympathy', *Philosophy* (1955).

ÁRDAL, PÁLL S., *Passion and Value in Hume's Treatise*, University Press, Edinburgh 1966.

BAIN, ALEXANDER, *The Emotions and the Will*, Parker, London 1859.

BASSON, A. H., *David Hume*, Penguin Books, Harmondsworth 1958.

BROAD, C. D., *Five Types of Ethical Theory*, Routledge & Kegan Paul, London 1930.

BUTLER, JOSEPH, *Fifteen Sermons*, in *The Analogy of Religion and Fifteen Sermons*, Religious Tract Society, London 1881.

CAMUS, ALBERT, *The Plague*, Penguin Books, Harmondsworth 1960.

COPLESTON, F., *A History of Philosophy*, Image Books, New York 1964.

GREEN, T. H., *Works*, edited by R. C. Nettleship, Longmans Green, London 1885.

HENDEL, C. W., *Studies in the Philosophy of David Hume*, Bobbs-Merrill, New York 1963.

HUDSON, W. D. (ed.), *The Is–Ought Question*, Macmillan, London 1969.

HUME, DAVID, *A Treatise of Human Nature*, edited by L. A. Selby-Bigge, Clarendon Press, Oxford 1888.

—— *Enquiries Concerning the Human Understanding and Concerning the Principles of Morals*, edited by L. A. Selby-Bigge, 2nd ed., Clarendon Press, Oxford 1902.

—— *Essays: Moral, Political and Literary*, University Press, Oxford 1963.

—— *Letters*, edited by J. Y. T. Grieg, Clarendon Press, Oxford 1932.

HUNTER, G., 'Hume on "Is" and "Ought"', *Philosophy* (1962).

KANT, IMMANUEL, *Groundwork of the Metaphysic of Morals*, in *The Moral Law*, translated by H. J. Paton, Hutchinson, London 1956.

KEMP SMITH, NORMAN, *The Philosophy of David Hume*, Macmillan, London 1941.

KENNY, ANTHONY, *Action, Emotion and Will*, Routledge & Kegan Paul, London 1963.

KROOK, DOROTHEA, *Three Traditions of Moral Thought*, University Press, Cambridge 1959.

KYDD, RACHAEL M., *Reason and Conduct in Hume's Treatise*, University Press, Oxford 1946.

LAIRD, JOHN, *Hume's Philosophy of Human Nature*, Methuen, London 1932.

LE BON, GUSTAVE, *The Crowd*, Unwin, London 1903.

MACLAGAN, W. G., 'Respect for Persons as a Moral Principle', *Philosophy* (1960).

MACMURRAY, JOHN, *Reason and Emotion*, Faber & Faber, London 1957.

MACNABB, D. G. C., *David Hume: his Theory of Knowledge and Morality*, 2nd ed., Blackwell, Oxford 1966.

NOWELL-SMITH, P. H., *Ethics*, Penguin Books, Harmondsworth 1954.

ROUSSEAU, JEAN JACQUES, *The Social Contract*, Dent 1941.

SCHELER, MAX, *The Nature of Sympathy*, translated by P. L. Heath, Routledge & Kegan Paul, London 1954.

SCHOPENHAUER, ARTHUR, *On the Basis of Morality*, translated by E. F. J. Payne, Bobbs-Merrill, New York 1965.

SCHWEITZER, ALBERT, *Christianity and the Religions of the World*, Allen & Unwin, London 1923.

SIDGWICK, HENRY, *The Methods of Ethics*, 7th ed., Macmillan, London 1907.

SMITH, ADAM, *The Theory of Moral Sentiments*, in *British Moralists*, edited by L. A. Selby-Bigge, Bobbs-Merrill, New York 1964.

STEPHEN, LESLIE, *Science of Ethics*, Smith Elder, London 1882.

STEWART, JOHN B., *The Moral and Political Philosophy of David Hume*, Columbia University Press, New York 1963.

WAND, BERNARD, 'A Note on Sympathy in Hume's Moral Theory', *Philosophical Review* (1955).

WILLEY, BASIL, *The Eighteenth-Century Background*, Penguin Books, Harmondsworth 1962.

WILLIAMS, B. A. O., *Morality and the Emotions*, Bedford College, University of London, 1965.

WILSON, JOHN, WILLIAMS, NORMAN, and SUGARMAN, BARRY, *Introduction to Moral Education*, Penguin Books, Harmondsworth 1967.

WITTGENSTEIN, LUDWIG, *Philosophical Investigations*, translated by G. E. M. Anscombe, 2nd ed., Blackwell, Oxford 1963.

INDEX